DIVORCE,
CHICAGO STYLE

DIVORCE,
CHICAGO STYLE

Tales of Love
(aNd Hate)
as Witnessed by a Divorce Attorney

Larry Ben Avraham

GOLDSMITH PUBLICATIONS

DISCLAIMER

I have tried to recreate events, locales, and conversations from my memory of them. In order to maintain anonymity, the names of individuals and places, as well as some identifying characteristics and details, have been changed. Accordingly, I have adopted an alias so that the people who read this book do not see themselves in the pages and sue me.

ISBN 978-0-692-79893-5

Library of Congress Control Number: 2016958647

Printed in the United States of America

Cover and book design by Mary Jo Zazueta

First Edition

To those married and divorced people...
I hope this book gives you a chance to laugh, cry, and learn.

Contents

Section VIII
ALL Divorces Require Difficult Decisions

Section IX
It's All About the Money, Honey

Preface

*Or, why this isn't exactly what my parents
had in mind when they sent me to college!*

I was the geek who sat in the front row throughout high school. The guy who actually loved going to math and science classes. When push came to shove and I decided on a college major, nobody had to twist my arm to steer me toward finance and the law. My parents, as you can imagine, were thrilled.

Over time, I practiced my craft and became a well-respected attorney and financial forensic Certified Public Accountant. However, nothing in my professional past could have properly prepared me for what I encountered when I began to specialize in counseling and advising Chicagoans embroiled in testy divorce actions. Talk about transformations. Adults morphed from loving couples to well-trained pit bulls specializing in everything from jugulars to asset grabbers extraordinaire.

These toxic adventures became so pervasive, I began keeping a record of the untoward and sometimes unbelievable things people inflicted on each other when marriages soured and vengeance replaced love. Along the way, I realized that these stories, while unbelievable in some cases, made perfect fodder for this book, which is how it came to be written.

Is Chicago different from other major metropolitan cities in the U.S.? I'm not sure because I only practice here, but I can unequivocally say that in Chicago, divorce is played for keeps.

It is brutal and sometimes lethal. Divorce is a universally painful process. It is emotional and gut wrenching. The parties, and sometimes the attorneys, increase the level of pain because it is easy to be sucked into cycles of revenge made sweeter by pain and blood.

In this collection of actual events, I have tried to describe my experiences while exploring the dark side of divorce and marital relations. Only someone who walks in the shoes of a divorcing couple can empathize with and understand their misery—with the exception of other jaded and cynical divorce attorneys.

I understand that unhappily married people experience sleepless nights. They watch meaningless television at all hours to help pass time, hour after hour. I see what my clients look like the next morning, when they arrive wearing a faux smile and hoping they won't burst into tears without provocation.

Some play the divorce game to punish and achieve revenge; others simply seek happiness. Only after my own divorce did I understand the word *peace*; which is why my personal life experience impacts my approach as I work with people running a gauntlet that is often similar to the one I endured.

Many of my clients long to obtain a divorce so they can find a special person the second time around with whom to share their heart and soul. They want to find out what it's like to be in a relationship with a true soul mate—be part of a union capable of providing the heat and passion of a relationship that lasts forever.

Within the pages of this book, I tried to shed light on what happens behind closed doors and the many reasons why people seek a divorce. You will read about a variety of spouses who, out of anger and hatred, practicality and need, behaved in shameful ways. It is my hope that the fictional characters (based on real ones) offer you wisdom, food for thought, and cautionary tales. If not, we attorneys are more than happy to take your money.

Acknowledgments

I want to thank my wife, Mary Ellen, who simply shook her head when I told her I was going upstairs to write this book. During the two-year process, she gave me her blessing, her love, and her encouragement. Thank you, Mary Ellen.

I would also like to thank Gail Cohen, who assisted me by breathing life into these stories.

Section 1

We Just Can't Stay Married

Marriage is More Than Sex

You've probably heard the phrase "No one knows what goes on behind closed doors." I've come to believe that this sentiment was first uttered to describe married life. We all have friends who, on the surface, seem to have splendid marriages and happy children. We witness spouses being tender and loving to each other; so it's easy to see why outsiders would easily conclude that the health of the marriage is good too.

But such facades are easily compared to ice cream subjected to hot sun: by the time things start going south, the neighborhood gossip machine is busy churning out stories of affairs, addictions, and abuses; so unless neighbors live under rocks, they become part of the gossip that chronicles what was once a good marriage.

That is exactly what happened to my clients Alice and Saul a few years ago. Things broke down. The usual suspects bantered back and forth to set the conditions for the divorce. On one particularly frosty Chicago morning, Alice and Saul ambled into the courthouse wearing wrinkled clothing, just in time for their

11:30 final meet-up with the judge who would, on that morning, end their three-year marriage. I was already there, impatiently tapping my foot and repeatedly checking the hands of my watch which moved at the speed of an old bottle of catsup.

Attorneys in place, we were ready to go. The disposition of the Alice-and-Saul matter looked to the judge like it was going to be a cakewalk because they had no children; thus removing one of the most contentious elements of any divorce action. But from the moment we arrived at the bench, I knew something was amiss. The judge peered down at all parties from behind her glasses.

You would have had to have been as close to the judge as I was to notice her eyes grow wide. The telltale aroma of booze reached the judge's nose just about the time it hit mine. The opposing attorney and I exchanged cautionary glances that said, "Better cancel our noon lunch dates."

The judge looked at the pair skeptically. "Have you two been out drinking all night?"

Giant grins spread across Alice's and Saul's faces. They checked out their feet in unison before nodding to the affirmative.

"So, were you two drinking together?" My counterpart and I began blinking in unison.

"Yup," Alice admitted, at which point Saul tried to muffle the giggle that the alcohol prompted.

The judge asked, "Are the two of you sober enough to be here today? Can you both understand the actions that you have requested the Court to grant you both?"

They both said yes in unison, again.

"Have you two had marital relations in the last nine months?" asked the judge.

Alice was taken aback by the question, responding, "What do you mean by 'marital relations'?"

Highly accomplished at the art of stopping an eye roll before it could begin, the judge clarified her question. "When did you two last have sex?"

Saul couldn't stop the blush that spread across his cheeks,

starting out as a pink flush that morphed into full-blown scarlet. Silence.

"Did you hear my question?" the judge queried in a no-non-sense tone that meant business.

Alice elbowed Saul but it was obvious that he wasn't going to answer; so rather than end up in jail for contempt—after all, there wasn't an episode of *Law & Order* Alice hadn't seen at least twice—she whispered, "This morning. I think."

Alice's answer was uttered so quietly, even her attorney asked her to repeat the answer so the judge and the court reporter could record the answer.

As it was the end of the morning and the judge guessed that this case had the potential to drag on thanks to the couple's col-lective state of inebriation, she said, "I am dying to know why the two of you want a divorce."

Quickly and emphatically, the couple blurted out their response in unison, "We need to be divorced!"

"You *need* to be divorced? Could one—or both—of you clarify your need for a divorce, because to be honest, I don't see anything that comes close to *need* in your relationship. In my opinion, if the sex is good, the marriage is good."

At this point, the entire courtroom of people leaned forward in obvious anticipation of the answer to the riddle that would solve this puzzle.

Alice took a deep breath. "Well, it's like this your honor. We verbally argue and fight about most subjects. The only things we enjoy doing together are partying all night and getting drunk. When we fight or get drunk, the passion overtakes us both and the make-up sex is the only thing we enjoy in our marriage." She took another breath and added, "I have never met a man who can make my body climax so quickly and so often."

Were the judge's toes curling beneath her robes, I wondered? Was she engaged in her own fantasy, now that Alice had opened this sensuous can of worms?

Of course, nobody would be privy to the judge's thoughts,

even me; though speculation pervaded the courtroom. The judge looked at Saul, who shoved his hands into his pockets. "It's true," he said. "The sex is great, and Alice is amazing, but frankly, I can't continue to live with her. I can't go to work and function if we fight in the morning or if we drink heavily the night before."

Saul's statement emboldened Alice. "Your honor, in the last three years, I was hoping that my husband would settle down, be a responsible husband, and want to start a family, but in truth, he always acts either like a stray dog or a bad puppy. I am tired of cleaning up his messes. I will most definitely miss the sex, but sex alone is not a good enough reason to stay married."

At last, said the look on the judge's face. Somebody is making sense. The judge looked down at her desk, entered some notes into the computer, turned her thoughts to lunch, and granted the divorce petition.

My Children Told Me To

Sometimes you just have to shake your head and wonder why a couple like the Goldbergs seek a divorce at this juncture in their lives. Even a conservative guess would set each of their ages at ninety-something; so it was with a mix of sadness and disbelief that Sylvia's son called me to handle Sylvia's side of her divorce from his dad, Sidney.

I was already in the courtroom when Sidney was wheeled in by his caregiver, past rows of seats, tables set up for attorneys, and the usual amount of courtroom clutter. The wheelchair made clicking noises as it awkwardly made its way into the well. Sidney's head leaned to one side. A cheery, red-plaid blanket had been thrown over his lap to keep him warm in the air-conditioned courtroom. I wondered if the blanket had been bought just for this occasion, but dared not ask.

Following in the wake of Sidney's wheelchair came Sylvia Goldberg, cane in hand, adding a tap-tap-tap sound to the courtroom's soundtrack. Nevertheless, she looked dignified, resolute, and purposeful as she joined the party being held at the bench that would forever end their sixty-plus years of marriage.

I have heard of couples in this age bracket seeking divorces because one of the spouses suffered from dementia and became violent, but I didn't have to watch Sidney very long to conclude that he was incapable of violence. From my perspective, he seemed oblivious to his surroundings, and was not hardly in good enough shape to spring from his chair, even if someone yelled, "Fire!"

I turned my attention to the judge. From where I was sitting, she didn't appear to be in good humor. Perhaps she was having a bad day. Maybe she was emotionally exhausted. After all, the woman spends her days adjudicating matters that affect lives. In my book, that earns a judge the right to look weary on occasion. I suspected that she had already listened to her fair share of cheating spouses, abuse, and sundry depressing tales that morning. Rumor had it she was recently offered a transfer to preside over commercial litigation matters, but chose to stay in Family Court because she thought she could make a difference.

Today appeared to be one of those days when she regretted that decision, big time.

Having spent plenty of time in this judge's court, I wasn't surprised to see her honor shake her head in disbelief as this geriatric parade appeared before her. She couldn't help but notice the way Sylvia's hand tenderly reached over to adjust Sidney's blanket each time it shifted or slipped. Such actions couldn't help but pull the heartstrings of everyone who witnessed each caress.

How obvious was it to everyone that love still remained between them? There wasn't a single person who wasn't wondering, "After so many years of marriage, why would this couple want to live their remaining last few years apart?"

Putting on her best professional demeanor, the judge had no choice but to subject the couple to the usual questions she posed before granting a dissolution of marriage. She knew that many of the questions were probably moot, and some may even be inappropriate, given their ages. But a mix of curiosity and perhaps the chance for some comic relief in the offing urged her forward.

"Are you here for a divorce?" This ice-breaker question was routine, but it was barely out of the judge's mouth before her honor realized it was obvious that the wife was hard of hearing. Sylvia stared motionless at the judge. I tried to intervene by speaking up to repeat the question and answer for the couple, since Sylvia was paying me to represent her interests.

The judge aimed her gaze directly at me. "I appreciate your counsel, but I want both parties to answer for themselves." She focused her eyes on Sylvia and asked the question for a third time in a louder and slower manner.

"Mrs. Goldberg, when was the last time you had marital relations with your husband?"

"Had what?"

"Your honor…" I chimed in. Obviously I was no longer using my indoor voice because once again I managed to get the attention of just about everyone in the courtroom. Most had moved to the edge of their seats, waiting for Sylvia's reply to the question.

"Not for a long time," Sylvia finally answered.

"Mrs. Goldberg, are you currently pregnant?"

I have to admit that even I was taken aback when the judge posed the question. At that point, quiet laughter pervaded the entire courtroom as the question was repeated for the benefit of Mrs. Goldberg.

Upon hearing the question for the second time, Sylvia's expression changed dramatically. Her eyes morphed from tired to merry as her cheekbones rose. She started laughing hysterically. "You're kidding me, right?"

The judge smiled before turning her attention to Sidney, who was completely oblivious to the jovial tone that now permeated the courtroom. He continued to stare ahead in a state of cluelessness. And as I watched the proceedings continue to their inevitable conclusion—the judge granted their dissolution of marriage request—I couldn't help but wonder what she was thinking when she took her recess after concluding what seemed to be pretty sad business.

I joined the throng in the hallway outside of the courtroom. Sylvia, Sidney, and their entourage emerged and were escorted to a gaggle of people awaiting them. Quite frankly, the atmosphere was jovial given the seriousness of the situation. I'm not beyond eavesdropping; so I sidled over and learned that these were the couple's children (kids eligible for Medicare, but children nevertheless!). They greeted their parents and learned that the divorce, based on irreconcilable differences, had been granted. Oddly, everyone seemed relieved.

Call me nosy, but I had to know what was going on; so I asked one of the Goldberg children to explain things to me. Amazingly, he was happy to fill me in. What the judge didn't know at the time—but may have suspected—was that Sidney did suffer from an advanced stage of dementia and required medical care around the clock. The couple had few resources, Sylvia was physically unable to care for her husband, and his medical care was projected to cost around $100,000 per year.

The divorce, explained the son, would allow the family to apply for Medicaid assistance for their father. The state would cover Sidney's medical bills and allow Sylvia to keep her condominium and some savings so she could continue to pay her bills. Sylvia knew that Sidney would get good care in the nursing home and she planned to visit him as often as the kids could drive her there.

Sidney had always promised to care for and watch over Sylvia. By undertaking this extreme legal action, he made good on his commitment. While they may no longer sleep together or share the life they once enjoyed, what the judge gave them was an irreplaceable gift: peace of mind.

I Want the Life You Promised Me

A sixty-year-old man named Sam came into my office. He was as talkative as a life insurance or car salesman, but very pleasant. Sam came to me because his business had suffered a financial reversal and now the Internal Revenue Service had come calling.

As I listened to him and reviewed the mass of paperwork he had schlepped to the appointment, I realized that Sam's debt was substantial, much of it due to several years of unpaid employee payroll taxes. When the recession hit and times got tough, Sam had chosen to finance the company's operations and his personal lifestyle using employee payroll tax withholdings. Time had gotten away from him, and he was now a target of the IRS.

Accompanying Sam to my office was his wife, Joan. I didn't find out until later that Sam was using our appointment to break the news to Joan that the business was in a near critical state and that he owed substantial tax obligations to the IRS.

Was this the first time a client had decided to declare me

Switzerland when breaking overwhelming financial news to a spouse? No. I could think of things I'd rather be doing, but I was his representative, after all.

This news came as a shock to Joan, who was the first to admit that she was clueless when it came to the business. She had no idea they had been living on borrowed funds for the past few years. As a stay-at-home spouse who enjoyed regular lunches with friends, impulse purchases, and weekly card games with the girls, she had no clue that things had become so bad. Sam had even worked out payment arrangements with the IRS agent now serving as his probation officer overseeing compliance.

By the time the two of them left my office, Joan was in such a state of shock, she was literally speechless—but according to Sam later, that didn't last farther than the parking lot adjacent to my office. She began firing on all cylinders during what must have felt like a year-long drive back to their home.

Sam recounted her tirade after they arrived home (safely). Joan had been counting down the years to when they would sell the business and purchase a house in Naples, Florida. She expected to maintain a summer condominium in downtown Chicago. She envisioned beach-front property with financial security and extensive world travel. "Now," she yelled at him, "those dreams are dust in the wind."

When Sam and I next met, he told me that, with each passing day, Joan grew angrier and more depressed. She refused to listen to what Sam had to say about the immediate steps they had to take to protect as many of their assets as possible. He insisted that I talk with Joan. He handed me the phone and now the onus was on me to inform her that they had to sell their home to downsize and that any unprotected savings (like retirement accounts) could be grabbed by the IRS.

"Sell our house?!" I had to move the phone away from my ear as she went into a rant worthy of the most skilled politician on the floor of Congress given leave to filibuster a contentious issue. "I promised to help the kids out!" she added when the topic of her home sale had run the gamut. "Now I can't help them either!"

I tried to interject a consoling word, but she just kept going. "What about the grandchildren? I wanted to spoil them! Can't you see what you're doing to me?"

"You don't have any grandchildren," I managed to slip in.

"But I will have them some day," she insisted. "And I'll have to say no to them, thanks to Sam's lousy business sense. I'm so embarrassed! My life is a train wreck."

It's been my experience that people react to financial threats in any number of ways. Joan, I concluded, was taking one of my favorites: It was all about her. Not a word mentioned about what Sam was going through after having lost his business, which can be like a death in the family for anyone who has spent his life building it. I took pity on Sam, but getting his house in order was up to him.

A couple of months passed after this conversation with Joan. I was concerned, so I called Sam. He confided that the tax situation had caused his wife to slip into a deep depression. Prescribed medications seemed to have little to no success improving her condition.

"Some nights," Sam explained in a hushed tone, "if she fails to take her medications, she can become violent. On a few occasions, she grabbed a large kitchen knife with serrated edges and swore she would kill me."

Fearing for Sam's life, I suggested he may want to try another doctor, move out for a while, or at the very least get rid of the knives; but all he could say was that he still loved Joan and hoped that they could return to the loving relationship they had enjoyed over the life of their marriage.

Obviously, Sam was assuming all responsibility for their financial predicament, and there was nothing I could say that would help. His plan of action was to continue on and hope he lived to get through this horrific time. What I wanted to say was, "Sam, if you had confided in Joan years ago and advised her about how things were falling apart financially, there's a chance that neither of you would be going through this."

Was he the first guy who consulted me about a financial crisis in which he tried to protect both his business and his wife from knowing the truth? Hardly. Fact is, Sam's wife hated the fact that she married a man who failed to be the person she thought he would become. She hated the fact that of the suitors she dated forty years earlier—each of whom became successful—she married the one who turned out to be a financial failure.

Sam did not fight Joan on the divorce. The total of the business and personal tax obligations was so great that the amount Joan was eligible to receive in court-ordered maintenance was severely limited. She wanted a healthy settlement so she could get some plastic surgery and meet someone wealthy and generous.

I wasn't able to tell Joan that the clients I work for, who are between the ages of sixty and sixty-five, make no apologies about seeking women who are ten to twenty years younger than they.

Sam worked like crazy to pay down his debt. He was able to re-launch and restore his business and achieve a nice level of profitability once the economy improved. In the near future, he hopes to have his tax debt fully paid off.

I check in with him off and on to find out how he's doing. The last time I called, Sam was dating a pretty, young woman. I always make it a point not to ask if he knows how Joan is doing because I happen to like the tone of his voice when he tells me about his successes these days!

Man Plans; the Angels Laugh

Harold traveled to the University of Illinois in Champaign-Urbana to meet and find love with the girl next door. Although they had attended the same high school and had a few classes together, their circle of friends never overlapped; so it took a sociology class at the University of Illinois to play matchmaker. One afternoon, Harold mentioned driving home to Northbrook to see his parents.

"Can I come?" Amy begged.

"Might not be enough room," he laughed.

She pouted sweetly.

"Okay, you can come. As a matter of fact, I'd welcome your company on the drive."

There's something about a road trip that brings out the person behind the mask. It took no time at all for Amy's true personality to come out and he was amazed that she was so agile when it came to saying things just for the shock value they provoked.

"You know, I was once arrested and served six months in jail for stealing tampons at Walgreen's." She delivered the announcement with such assurance, his foot went to the brake.

"Seriously?"

"Eyes on the road, Harold—10 and 2," she added, referring to where hands belonged at the wheel of a car. "You're so gullible." Although the drive was less than three hours, they decided to stop for lunch. Amy agreed to pay for the gas while he would pay for lunch. Upon reaching Amy's parent's house, she jumped out of the car, dragged bags of laundry out of his trunk, and gave Harold a kiss on the cheek.

Later in the evening, Amy texted him. "What's up? Want to grab lunch tomorrow?"

"Sure," he responded, to which Amy added this playful response: "What are you wearing?"

"Why do you ask?"

"Because I want to make sure you're not texting me naked."

He was intrigued and responded in kind, whereupon she sent him a snapshot of herself in flannel pajamas.

"Wow, I need a cold shower, Amy."

This was the first time the couple began to indulge in sexual play and, as most relationships that shift in this direction do, hormones kicked in and the banter grew suggestive.

The next day, they met up for hot dogs and Amy brazenly wiggled her meat, suggesting it would be difficult to put something this long down her throat. As Harold sat there speechless, she added, "I hope you're not this big."

Once they were off and running on this line of conversation, it was just a matter of time before the two enjoyed their first make-out session. By the time they headed back to the university, it wasn't a matter of whether they would have sex but how soon.

The University of Illinois campus looked decidedly different when the pair returned to town. From that moment on, they were inseparable and Harold fell into a state of bliss when he learned how experimental Amy was willing to be when the two were in bed. She obviously had more experience and Harold was content to be her student.

During their sophomore year, Amy and Harold rented an apartment off campus. The pair split expenses and shared all chores with the exception of one: Harold was not allowed to do Amy's laundry after he managed to turn all of her underwear blue.

By senior year, the two acted like an old married couple—spats and all—and as the days wound down to graduation and companies came to campus to recruit top seniors for job openings, Harold and Amy both received offers from prestigious Chicago-based companies. The pair was eager to find an apartment to make their transitions complete, landing in a trendy neighborhood that appealed to young couples. All that was left was the inevitable; so Amy asked the question: "So, when are we getting married?"

Breaking the news to both sets of parents at a popular suburban Chicago restaurant, the couple was giddy and the wine that flowed, courtesy of both fathers who kept up a constant banter about which one would be the most honored to pick up the check. There was much discussion about which month worked best for the wedding.

Time flew by as the couple was immersed in settling into new jobs and wedding planning, but at last, the big day arrived and the event was splendid. Because their work schedules were tight, they put off a tropical honeymoon until later that year, instead they settled for a resort in Wisconsin where a quaint cabin outfitted with every modern amenity was their haven for a blissful weekend.

Reluctant to leave, they nevertheless packed and drove back to Chicago late in the day after getting in a final river rafting adventure. Feeling blissful and content, Harold turned the car south, hoping to get home by midnight. Amy was snuggled against him for the ride. Like most unexpected experiences, he realized too late that they were heading directly into the path of a huge stag.

Harold awoke in a hospital. He felt for a call button and rang for a nurse, eager to know about Amy. An on-call doctor responded and told him not to worry. Amy had been taken to a trauma center specializing in head injuries. Harold needed to spend another night for observation and couldn't get to her, but he arranged for his brother to pick him up the following morning so he could be at her bedside.

Still aching and wearing a few bandages, Harold went straight to the ICU unit where he found her parents. They told him that she had already had two surgeries to relieve pressure on her brain and that she was in a medically induced coma to allow her body to start healing. Nobody on her medical team knew the full extent of the injuries she sustained.

Harold sat next to his unconscious wife. He talked about their future as she lay there motionless, tubes and pumps pumping fluids in and out of her body. Hours turned to days. He slept in a chair when sleep claimed him, and returned home only to shower and change clothes before returning to her bedside.

After two weeks, doctors performed brain scans and tests to determine the extent of her brain damage and the news was bad: Amy would never regain her mental faculties. She was placed in a therapeutic facility as Harold and Amy's families were forced to return to their daily lives. At first, Harold was at her bedside daily. Over time, he visited less and less, until he agreed with her family and doctors that taking her off life support was the only good option.

This, sadly, is where I came in. Harold retained me to represent him in a divorce action after Amy's father sat him down and explained that Amy wouldn't want him to remain chained to her. He appreciated his father-in-law's words, but it still took a long time for Harold to ask me to file those papers.

In the end, he came to my office with his father-in-law. I was touched by the way these two men had come to terms about the woman they both loved most. As for me, I couldn't help but speculate why, in light of all of the contentious divorces I had handled for decades, this loving couple couldn't have had more time together.

How do You Define a Good Marriage?

Jeff and Summer were married for over thirty-five years. Like many couples, they had their good years and their not-so-good years. I worked with Summer for the last fifteen years when she was my office manager. As it goes in most offices, we had many casual conversations, but I wasn't expecting her to talk with me about personal matters, mostly because she always seemed to be a private person when it came to her marital affairs.

I let her talk because she seemed to have nobody she felt comfortable confiding in. She explained that over the past few years, she had become a different person, ever since her mom, who was also her best friend, was diagnosed with cancer. Treatments didn't work, and the family was informed that she had about six months left.

Fed up with surgeries that had not bought her extra time, Summer's mom finally announced that she was ready to die rather than having her body carved up again like a Thanksgiving Day turkey. She was a proud woman who wanted to die with dignity, and she did just that.

It felt good to help Summer through this difficult time and, given the fact that we had gotten closer, I confided I was writing this book and asked her for insights on how to define a good marriage. Her eyes grew wide and she asked if I had plans that night. I called my wife, told her I was having dinner with Summer, and would fill her in when I got home.

I had a hunch we'd be talking about everything but my manuscript, but I certainly couldn't complain since I was the person who posed the question about her viewpoint on good marriages. We went to a quiet restaurant near my office.

I broke the ice by asking, "So, to what do you attribute the success and longevity of your marriage?" It was a standard question I asked of clients.

Her response was revealing. "I accept the fact that my husband, in his own way, loves me. He's not as physical as I might like," she added, sipping her wine.

"Was this an issue you found difficult to deal with?" I asked.

"Actually, when I talked to my friends, I learned that their husbands weren't exactly sex crazed, either."

I laughed aloud and relaxed a bit, until she added, "I want to share something personal with you and I don't want you to ever discuss this with anyone else."

As an attorney, I was used to making such promises—after all, if I had a big mouth, I don't think I would last long in this business. I nodded my head and she began.

"I love Jeff," she began, "but he hadn't the capacity to meet my needs. Sometimes, I needed sex. Other times, I just needed physical closeness; hugging and cuddling. I suffered quietly, starved for attention, because he is the father of my children and I knew in his way he loved us."

The food arrived but I didn't pick up my fork out of deference to Summer, who had more to say.

"My mother was a special woman. We called each other daily and considered each other best friends, which meant we could talk about everything under the sun. Even when she got her cancer diagnosis, I couldn't accept it because her personality was so strong. I thought she could beat the odds and live forever."

Summer urged me to eat before my food got cold, so I ate as she kept talking. "When I was confronted with the reality of my mom's death, I felt so alone I couldn't seem to come out of it and no therapist was able to bring me out of my funk. I begged my husband but, again, he had no clue how to comfort me"

"I grew angry and moved into our daughter's old bedroom six months ago. I tried therapy again, and this counselor had me write letters to Jeff to release my anger. She said, 'You don't ever have to send them, but it could help to write them and put them away.' So, I did.

"But one night—and don't ask me why I did it—I handed those letters to Jeff and he was dumbfounded. I told him how much anger had consumed me when he denied me the support I so badly needed as my mom was dying. Know what his answer was? 'You're strong. I knew that you would get over it without my help.'

"That was the moment I knew I could never forgive him for all of those years when I felt alone and unloved. Even as I fought for my sanity while dealing with my dying mother, he was nowhere to be found. This is the man I expected to grow old with and share a future." Summer took a long drink of her wine and a big grin spread across her face. "You want to know my view on how to define a good marriage?"

I nodded.

"Having the guts to tell the truth, as I did when I showed Jeff those letters and realized at that moment I didn't have a good marriage. That's why I wanted to talk to you. Can I retain you? I've had enough. No regrets. But I'm not going to live without physical and emotional love for another day."

I gave Summer my "favorite client" rate to celebrate her new-found freedom. Last I heard, she had gone online and found a great guy, although her profile reads: "No interest in marriage."

That will change. It always does!

To Sleep, Perhaps to Snore

When Rachel barged into my office for the first time, I had the feeling I was going to get an earful just by the way she entered, grabbed a seat, and plopped down in front of me.

I had barely taken out the query sheet I use to take notes about a new client's case.

"He's killing me," she said in a strident tone.

"Who is killing you?" It seemed the natural response.

"My husband. Herb. He snores so much, I haven't slept in years, and I can't take it anymore."

"You want a divorce on the grounds that your husband's snoring has gone on too long? How long have you two been married?"

"Forty years last August."

"Has your husband tried to get some help?"

"You name it, we've tried it. Nose clips. A mask hooked up to a machine. Sleep clinic. We spent a fortune on a bed so he could sleep in an elevated position."

My secretary had peeked in to remind me of something and was now holding her hand over her mouth to keep from laughing. I beckoned her in, she slipped me a note, and off she went.

"I would kill for a good night's sleep," Rachel said with a great emphasis on the word *kill*. Hmm. We seem to have a theme here. "The only answer is divorce," she said, "and that's why I am here."

"Well, as your potential legal representative, I should tell you that snoring has not yet been put on the list of grounds this county recognizes. Can you tell me what other complaints you have about your marriage?"

"Complaints? The man's a saint. He has always given me a great life—anything I would want. I never had to work and our kids adore him. I do, too. I just need to get some sleep."

"Can't you move him into another room and close the door?"

"He is in another room. Down the hall. Door closed. The older he gets, the worse the snoring. I'm not going to stay married to him unless he does something about it."

"What other options do you have?" I asked. "It sounds like you've already tried everything."

"I'm not giving up. I know there is an answer. I just want that answer to be him living in another place so I can get some sleep."

"You know, you can live apart and not get a divorce," I suggested.

"You don't want the business? I should find another lawyer," she said, starting to get up.

"I didn't say that, Rachel." Although I was thinking that another lawyer might be a better bet. You see, in the interest of transparency, my wife threatens to divorce me at least once a week due to my snoring, but I don't remember anything from law school that exonerates me from taking a case just because I happen to be in the same boat as Rachel's husband. "We need to figure out what grounds we can use, since snoring isn't an option."

"My husband says he wants to make me happy and that whatever you say, he is going to abide by it."

"Could I just suggest that one of you move out? I am happy to handle your divorce, but it really isn't necessary. You can spend the money you would have paid me to get another place."

Rachel thought a minute, thanked me for the free advice, and left.

I went home that night to beg my wife's forgiveness and asked her to make a list of things I can do to make her life a bit more tranquil at night. I did, however, inform her that I wasn't moving anywhere.

Life is Too Short

Stacy and Mark met at college, rented an apartment together, and moved back to Chicago to start their careers. They took an apartment in a three-story walk-up in an old building in East Rogers Park a blue-collar neighborhood. They were give his mom's old car and commuted on the "El" (train) to avoid the parking fees downtown. Their entry-level jobs were nondescript and lacked a future.

They married in a small ceremony with sixty of their friends and family in attendance. Mark and Stacy were under twenty-one and felt compelled to marry because that's what they thought they were expected to do. A month later, reality set in: they were married but they were broke, they hated their jobs, and they felt they lived under a dark cloud.

Stacy was Mark's first love. Yet he never learned the responsibilities that go along with the title husband. He remained selfish, incapable of putting Stacy's needs ahead of his own. He loved Stacy, she was his best friend, the first person he would call when good and bad things happened. She was the single person in his life with whom he could bare his soul and thoughts, during the day or during pillow talk—but he rarely asked for her thoughts or feelings. She had the Irish glimmer in her eyes and the largest, perfect smile. Her heart was made of sweet sugar, she was the person people would seek out to befriend.

Stacy adored Mark. He was everything she dreamed of: he was handsome, her best friend, and devoted to her. She grew up in a traditional blue-collar family. Her mother, a housewife, emotionally supported her husband and had dinner on the table as his car pulled into the driveway. She knew Mark needed maturing but, like her mother, failed to speak up.

Over the next five years, they purchased an ordinary garden-level condo in the burbs an hour from work. Mark traded jobs several times without finding his calling; Stacy found great employment with a law office where she was appreciated.

I met Mark on a Saturday, at a park district intermediate tennis class. He had a great serve and was quite competitive. After several classes, we went together to the hot dog stand and enjoyed a refreshing juice drink or two while discussing sports and careers. Always promoting my services, he seemed intrigued and began to ask questions, as if he was a consumer.

I cut to the chase and asked, "Mark, are you happily married?"

He seemed befuddled by the question. So I began to ask him the following questions:

"Do you love your wife?"

A long drawn out yes.

"Do you enjoy your sex life together?"

A quicker yes, with a smirk.

"Does your wife enjoy your sex life?"

He bit his lip and said, "I think so."

"Do you or have you had an affair?"

"Don't most guys?"

"Are you happy?"

His face grew somber and he answered, "No."

"Do you want children?"

"Not now. We live paycheck to paycheck."

I realized he could not afford my fees; so I thought maybe I could help him repair his life by being the mentor he sought. I suggested we go out to a movie that night with our wives. In many ways, my wife is much wiser than I am; so I sought her insight to help this young couple.

While the boys were in line buying tickets, after the movie pizza, and during the girls' bathroom break, they talked and shared whatever women talk about. I kept it light with Mark, discussing the Bears chances in the playoffs and other sports nonsense that guys discuss.

In the car, I turned to my wife. She said, "I know what you are going to ask. Stacy is a sweet young girl. She wants children and wants to feel love in her life. She wants to be needed."

It seems Mark was consumed with the lack of money and he could not find his niche in life, which made him depressed and distant.

"Dear, this poor, sweet girl deserves better. She simply desires to be a mom. I am afraid she is with a boy trying to find himself."

"Wow! You gave me both barrels, as I knew you would."

The following week after tennis, I led the discussion but let Mark make his own decision. It was best in the long run for Stacy.

I Need a Divorce, But You Can Trust Me

To become a partner and to garnish the big dollars in the big firms, one must be willing to work sixty-hour weeks. I remember working on legal briefs in the delivery room. The sacrifices we make to achieve financial and professional success are shared by our spouses and children. Sometimes we do not realize the affect these long hours have on our families.

After a while, I decided life was too short and devoted time to living and family. I realized success was being with my family. My friend Sam chose financial security. As his professional star grew, his bank account expanded and his marriage suffered.

They had one child, who had medical issues. Julie found being a single parent daunting. Julie tried to be the best wife and mom. To her credit, she was supportive of Sam, being the caring, smiling wife at business events; the mom who attended every school event and helped their son with his studies at night. Julie sacrificed the life she envisioned for herself when she accepted the role of supportive wife and caregiver.

The years of giving led to depression, weight gain, and loss of sexual appetite. Sam expected a trophy wife when he arrived home in the late hours, a wife who wanted to please her man. Instead, he would find an exhausted woman needing to talk.

In the early days, Julie was a looker. But like most of us, over the years, she gained weight which erased her good looks. Sam worked out with a trainer and played golf regularly and appeared to be in great shape. To attract new clients, he joined a country club and met with clients and prospective clients after work for dinner and drinks. Sam became the man whom Julie simply shared a bed with.

The perks of this earned wealth: the vacations, the club, and the things one can purchase, unfortunately did not include happiness. Sam wanted more from his wife, more than she was capable of giving.

Sam graciously invited me to play as a regular in his Saturday morning foursome. In the golf cart, we would talk. He seemed to always be willing to discuss his perceived bad marriage and unhappiness. I tried to understand why he was unhappy.

"Sam, how do you deal with your wife's weight gain? Does it bother you?"

"Lar, I have no desire to have her. She is so big that honestly the thought of it would make me sick."

I followed up with the obvious next question.

"Lar, there are a lot of women out there who are unhappy with their lives and people that I meet professionally who seek a relationship without strings or a commitment. Some of my late nights may be with someone other than a client."

He told me this as I approached the green to make a par putt from twenty-some feet away from the hole. Sam acted and dressed like the most conservative professional: two-piece designer suits and when asked a question, he would provide a slow, thoughtful professional answer. I would not expect him to be a playboy. I blew the putt.

Even with this information, I was surprised when I received a call asking me to represent Sam in his divorce. He had decided that since his son was in a good place and going off to college, maybe it was time to move on with his life.

Sam had sat down with Julie to work out the financial aspects, however she was in shock and no dollar amount would have repaid her for the pain she had suffered. Eventually, her attorney was able to assist in the negotiations and she received a generous settlement, one that exceeded what a judge would have deemed appropriate.

Sam had been dating openly for the last six months and when we would talk, he was enjoying his newfound freedom. Then, I received this call. "Lar." I heard tears in his voice. "Julie has been diagnosed with stage four cancer."

He shared with me that he was going to take time off as needed, move into the old marital residence, and care for Julie. For the next year, Sam drove her to appointments, fed her, and held her hand until such time as he handled her funeral arrangements. Julie assigned Sam to manage her estate for the benefit of their son.

Your Wife Has Teeth

Judd is that preacher's son who was expected to be on best behavior, dress well, and smile 24/7. Like most preachers' sons he had a quiet, wild streak. Around his parents, he was the obedient son. He loved his parents and would never hurt them.

Judd graduated from law school and moved back to Chicago, where he joined a boutique litigation firm. There he made a mark as a skillful litigator. His star power grew and he was considered for partnership—until he butted heads with a senior partner. He was right about the argument; he won the battle but lost the war. He would never be considered for a partnership position.

As a single man in Chicago with a nice income, Judd attracted the best lookers in the city. Many of the young women were loads of fun; though not the type of girls you bring home to meet parents. Judd was being pressured by his parents to date serious woman, someone his parents would consider suitable for

Marriage. He and his parents had different ideas as to what that girl would be like.

Judd sought to escape work and parental pressures by going to Jamaica for a week.

"Lar, do you want to join me? I am going to Hedonism II Resort in Jamaica."

"Judd, never heard of it .What kind of place is it?"

"Well, clothes are optional."

"Judd, while exciting, I cannot do it.

Judd stayed for a week in Hedonism, alone. The place was like summer camp. There was finger painting, but instead of wearing clothes you painted clothes on someone of the opposite sex using your fingers or a brush. There were ball games: nude volleyball. There were arts and crafts: you created sexual objects. There was time-out: you would go back to your hut with another person and have sex.

The first three days were exhausting. Judd entertained so many women and participated in so many activities he almost wanted an evening to recharge his batteries. Then, on the third evening, Judd saw Ronet as she was walking to the open bar, followed by countless eyes. Ronet was an amazingly beautiful woman, with more European than American features. Ronet too had gone there to escape her parents' pressures and to live out her sexual fantasies. Once Judd saw Ronet, he placed a target on her back and sought to make her his next conquest. The problem was he was not the only guy with his sights on Ronet.

He walked up to her just before another suitor started for her. He asked her to grab a bite, brash maybe, but he was a litigator. She accepted; they found much in common. Her parents were Old World immigrants; she endured a strict, rigid upbringing. Her parents wanted her to marry their friend's geeky son who excelled in math and wore pants that were too short. Her parents were controlling. Even at the age of twenty-six, she was expected to live at home until she married, and needed to announce where she was going and what time she would return home each evening. No wonder she needed this place to release her inhibitions.

As he told me the story, she was captivated by his sexual appetite and ability to please woman; so she stayed with him exclusively. After they returned home, Judd to Chicago and Ronet to Portland, Maine, they stayed in contact by phone. It took three weeks for Judd to fly to Portland, where he proposed.

Over the next ten years, they had three children, a house, and Judd had his own law practice. Being a preacher's son, the members of the congregation became a good feeder for his business. Ronet was his paralegal and legal secretary. Every weekend they had family dinners with Judd's parents. It seemed they had settled into the kind of marriage their parents envisioned.

Judd, like many attorneys, met with business prospects after work to promote and grow his business. Judd developed many of his clients at evening networking events. Judd's wildness did not go into hibernation for long. In fact, when the sex became stale at home, he ventured into cheating waters.

I came over to Judd's office one evening; it was about six. We were going to the club to play basketball after some dinner. His office doors were locked. I saw lights on through the glass doors and knew someone was there. I banged on the door and Judd emerged from the office with his pants unzipped and the summer secretary was buttoning her shirt as she came out of the room. She was doing more than dictation. "I assume that your other two attorneys went home early?"

In the summer, Ronet stayed home with the kids and the office hired a temporary secretary. This one was young and cute. During dinner, Judd explained that she was going through a rough time and required hand holding. I had a suspicion that Judd was an active player but lacked the physical evidence.

Later that year, it was winter, we walked along Rush Street to a restaurant, sat down at the table, when a brunette approached our table, kissed Judd, and sat down. I was soon to learn that Judd had fallen in love. I tried to hate this woman for destroying my friend's family, but her charm and sweetness owned me. She was an educated woman, a success in her profession, well-respected, and never married, with a heart of gold.

Judd told me that he had decided to move out of his home within the next sixty days and file for divorce. He asked if I would handle his matter. "Lar, I do not want to hurt Ronet. I want a fair settlement and do not want to hurt her more than I have already."

This woman had a calming effect on Judd, he was a changed man. She brought the best out in him. I loved Ronet as a friend, she was a good mother and a good wife, but their relationship did not have passion.

Two months passed and Judd moved out and then told his parents. His parents were not happy and refused to permit the new girlfriend to join them at the family dinner table. After about a month, Judd sat down with his mother, and they agreed Judd would return home to Ronet for thirty days. If after that time things could not be corrected, then Judd's parents would not interfere. Judd would not be permitted to talk or communicate with the girlfriend during that time. Judd's mother had consulted with Ronet before she made these arrangements; it was now up to Ronet.

Judd explained the deal to his new love. She agreed to wait, knowing that they would spend a lifetime together. She loved Judd but also understood the importance of family in his life.

The first few days, Ronet played it cool. When the kids asked questions about a possible breakup, Ronet forced Judd to handle that dirty job. The task brought tears to his eyes. Judd's parents added extra pressure by expressing their feelings that they preferred Ronet over the weekend dinners.

I received a phone call from Judd. "Lar, dismiss the petition for divorce."

"What happened?"

"I love my parents and realized that I love Ronet, and our family is special. Last week she reminded why I married her. She woke me up in the morning, she was on top of me riding me, and it was great sex."

I did not ask if he would have another affair. I wanted to believe he had learned his lesson.

Nine months later, Judd and Ronet had their fourth child, a beautiful girl.

Gentleman Jack

I was retained to investigate a cheating husband and was surprised by what I found. Normally my investigation begins with an interview with the spouse who retained me. It is a waste to begin an investigation without background information. It is almost comical that most of these hot cheaters have provided their spouses complete access to their Facebook, email, and checking accounts. In this case, the innocent spouse established the accounts, the passwords, and was able to provide me with complete access.

I asked Mandy, a southern lady from Texas, how she had met John, her husband. "He was my boss at the time. We worked for a Fortune 100 company in Houston. We became work buddies and then, one day, he sent white roses to my home. The card said 'Mandy, I know that it is inappropriate for me to ask one of my employees out on a date; however you are the most charming and beautiful woman I have ever known. I would appreciate it if you would join me after work Friday night at Sullivan steakhouse.'

"We had a wonderful dinner; he stood when I would stand, pushed in my chair, rushed to open my car door, and appeared interested in me. After the date, he sent me more roses. In fact, up until we split up, he would send me flowers every Friday. He still opened car doors for me and was the perfect gentlemen."

They had married in a small chapel in southeast Texas. John's brother performed the ceremony. She showed me a picture of her in her wedding dress; she was forty pounds lighter and was absolutely gorgeous. "During our ten years together, he would receive pleasure purchasing expensive jewelry for me and dressing me in the finest designer outfits. The evenings, when we were in town, we would enjoy the best and hottest restaurants in the city. We made a lot of money, so we did not care what we would spend."

John was transferred to Chicago; Mandy took a job in New York. They spent two weeks a month together, the rest of the time they traveled separately. Mandy began to get suspicious when she saw strange checks being written from the joint checking account. She hired a detective and learned that John had another family of sorts.

It appears John was a sexual addict for S&M. In each city, he would make it a point to locate the underground S&M joints. There, he would find an evening of sexual pleasure. In Chicago, his dominatrix was an Asian woman named May. Eventually John fell in love with May and her demanding ways.

The records we uncovered indicated that the affair lasted at least three years before Mandy learned of it. Throughout this time, he appeared to be a loving, faithful husband, sending flowers, calling Mandy during the day and at night to see how she was doing, and leaving her cards by the bed telling her that he would love her forever.

The affair began to unravel when John purchased a $20,000 watch for Mandy and the band did not fit her petite wrist; so she went to have links removed. When Mandy went to the jewelry store, the salesman, after finding two invoices, commented, "You are fortunate to have such a generous husband. He purchased you two beautiful pieces of jewelry." Mandy asked to see the invoices, she had received only one piece of jewelry. We later learned that May received the other piece of jewelry.

I asked why it took her so long to realize he was having an affair. "Lar, together we earn seven figures. I pay the credit card bills, the house expenses. I do not get caught up in the details. We always have six figures of cash in the bank accounts. Why would I question anything?"

For years, John ordered two sets of flowers to be delivered on Friday mornings. He purchased an apartment for May, a new bed, new furniture, and decided to financially support her so that she would not be required to practice her vocation with others. John had May accompany him on all his out of town trips too.

John's parents were ministers. Mandy began to laugh, with tears in her eyes. "I wonder what kind of work he will tell his parents she performs! I bet it's not the truth!"

I sat for an hour with Mandy. She was broken-hearted because she thought she had fallen for a real prince only to find that her prince was not real. Examining credit card statements, we found over one hundred thousand dollars of gifts for his paramour.

We noticed medical procedures that John had paid for: new teeth, breast modifications, and facial changes. As we located doctors who were paid from the credit card statements, we would Google their names to learn their specialty. It was easy to surmise the nature of the expenditure. We found Dr. Lilly Smithe's name and surmised that May may be pregnant.

At that point, Mandy broke down in tears and became a basket case. "Lar, that asshole told me he never wanted kids. Truthfully he was like a demanding child. I knew he would never share me with a child. I sacrificed my ability to have children and the dream of a family for him."

I consoled her as best as I could. Not being a woman, I cannot know the anguish she was feeling.

John had been sly. Over the last three years, he had part of his paycheck electronically deposited in their joint checking account with another portion of the check electronically deposited into another bank account at a different bank. The same with his six-figure year-end bonus check. Mandy never noticed the change in monies. John used the secret bank account to pay for May's upkeep and welfare.

When we finished our investigation, Mandy's attorney used the pregnancy to force a quick settlement. We uncovered possibly a half million dollars in expenditures and we found monies that were socked away for the benefit of the paramour. John paid Mandy monies to cover half of what he had spent on May and then agreed to pay Mandy a handsome financial settlement.

Unfortunately the pain that Mandy suffered is priceless and cannot be compensated by money. She will be seeing a shrink for years to come. I hope she finds a real Prince Charming; she truly is a good soul.

Money is the Root of All Evil

Sid and Kathy were married for ten years; had two young, bright, and fun-loving children in elementary school; and were very successful at everything they did because they were both good-looking, sweet, good people who were liked and trusted by the people with whom they did business. As their financial advisor, it was a pleasure being in their company. I looked forward to hearing about their children's accomplishments when we met.

Because they were such engaging people, Sid and Kathy had equally successful careers; both as self-employed clothing manufacturer representatives. I used to joke that it was because each of them ran their own showrooms at Chicago's Apparel Mart—consequently, both Sid and Kathy ruled their own fiefdoms, yet they managed to keep their marriage healthy!

As manufacturer representatives, the couple lived in the fast lane, dining and partying with department store buyers to secure orders for the upcoming season's fashions six months before they appeared in their showrooms. As a result, they wielded some power with the manufacturers who relied on advance orders to identify which garments were to be manufactured.

Because both of them were ambitious and eager to succeed professionally, they were in constant motion. Sid covered a huge Midwestern states territory. Kathy not only ran her Apparel Mart showroom but she also ran a trunk show business, selling clothing at home parties hosted by a clientele that consisted of many wealthy suburban women who loved getting the inside track on designer fashions at these exclusive get-togethers.

By skillfully running both businesses, purchasing $20,000 worth of clothing for her trunk shows was no big deal for Kathy. Sid frequently received job offers to manage sales divisions of brand-name clothing lines, which would require moving to Los Angeles—a prospect Kathy wanted no part of because her career was entrenched in Chicago, as were their children's lives.

If this introduction has led you to believe that few married couples were situated as nicely as Kathy and Sid were, I refer you back to what I stated in the Preface: in marriage, it is often the case that what you see on the surface is just an illusion.

Would it surprise you to learn that, despite being the picture of financial success, Sid and Kathy were usually penniless? When I make that statement, I am not exaggerating. The couple had zero savings and no funded retirement plans. They lived in the elite suburb of Glencoe, on Lake Michigan, in a house that cost well over a million dollars and the property was fully mortgaged. Ironically, Sid grew up in a family where fiscal responsibility was a virtue.

On the other hand, Kathy suffered from one of contemporary society's biggest addictions: she was incapable of controlling her spending habits. When she saw something, the urge to buy was overwhelming and she gave in to the urge every time it struck.

Sid and I were aware of the problem. At one point, things got so bad, I was able to talk Kathy into getting counseling for her addiction, but it didn't cure her problem for long. The couple always managed to pull out a save to avert the latest crisis: re-mortgage the house, get more cash from untapped credit cards, and synthesize debt. When in a pinch, they even borrowed from relatives, but the debt mounted like an African ant colony: one minute it was small and in the next, it dominated the landscape.

Like most crises that are repeatedly tamped down and never really fixed, neither Sid nor Kathy can recall to this day exactly why he snapped on that cool, fall day after their latest re-fi attempt was rejected by the lender due to a lack of equity. That evening, he literally exploded with vicious anger.

"One more financial spending spree and I am going to leave you!" he shouted. "I'm fed up and I can't spend another minute of my life chasing dollars to pay bills. We have two beautiful children and we haven't even put away money to send them off to college; nor do we have any credit. God forbid either of us get sick or injured. We have no savings."

Sid called me and told me about his ultimatum. I gave lip service to optimism, but frankly, neither of us acknowledged the 100-pound gorilla in the room. Meanwhile, Kathy blithely assumed that Sid would get over his snit and went into the city, as usual, to continue servicing her personal needs.

Sid took his shirts and two suits to the cleaners. Kathy usually handled the dry cleaning, but since he had time to run by the shop, this particular morning he tossed the cleaning into the car on his way to work.

"I'm really sorry," the clerk said when Sid placed his clothing on the dry cleaner's counter, "but unless you pay the outstanding balance on your account, I can't take these clothes."

"No problem," Sid said, feeling somewhat embarrassed as he slid a credit card out of his wallet. "What's the balance?"

"Well, it's $1,326."

"Are you joking?"

"No sir."

Sid demanded to see their account ledger and sure enough, a tab had been accruing for months without a single payment made on the balance.

After settling the bill with his credit card and feeling thankful that the card hadn't been rejected, Sid immediately went home and began to search the house for other surprises. While he was undertaking his search, the postman delivered the mail. Sid shuffled the envelopes and noticed credit card statements addressed only to Kathy.

That's when Sid discovered Kathy had opened several new charge accounts and was actively concealing new debt that she had amassed, in addition to the joint accounts he knew about. Furious, his hands began to sweat and tremble as he felt his face flush. It was the first time he ever recalled wanting to act violently. He knew enough to sit down and calm down before taking any action.

Sid called me and asked if we could meet in a couple of hours. My schedule was already packed, but he pleaded with me and refused to tell me why this meet-up was so urgent. I acquiesced and we agreed on a quiet place to meet for lunch. Meanwhile, Sid canceled his appointments.

As we sat across the lunch table from each other, I could tell that a tipping point had been reached. He disclosed as many details about their financial dilemma as he could and passed me a big manila envelope that was stuffed with statements. That day, he retained me to handle his divorce, since I was in the best position to represent him knowing, as I did, the family's financial history.

That evening, Sid told Kathy he was done and was filing for divorce. He told her that he loved her but she was killing him because of her financial irresponsibility. He could not to live any longer with someone who had no intention or desire to change. She knew her luck had run out and didn't say a thing. The next day, they broke the news to the children and he moved out.

Things moved fairly quickly at this point. Sid and Kathy worked out a co-parenting agreement. They agreed to a fair financial settlement and the court included it in their dissolution order: each was responsible for 50 percent of the debt created in the marriage and since both of their incomes were approximately the same, there would be no scheduled maintenance or child support required. The house was sold.

Sid now lives in Los Angeles with his daughter and son, and he enjoys financial security now that he is free of Kathy. I lost touch with her after learning that her businesses had failed. And because she was in such debt, she even asked Sid to take custody of both children until she could get her feet back on the ground.

Sid flies Kathy to Los Angeles twice a year to spend time with their children and he still keeps in touch with me via e-mails and the occasional phone call when he's in Chicago. There is a joy in his voice that I never heard until he broke free of his financial yoke. He always laughs and tells me that he has finally discovered what it's like to sleep all night without counting numbered sheep jumping over fences!

Your Soul Mate Might be Married

Jerry met Jan at a Chicago tavern and grill, mustered his courage, and approached her without an introduction! They talked for hours and realized they had plenty in common. They began dating that night and it wasn't long before Jerry knew that Jan was the perfect girl for him. She was athletic and enjoyed snorkeling and hiking. He could talk football and baseball with her and she knew her way around theatre talk, too. At home, she enjoyed the physicality of their relationship, which ran the gamut from raw sex to tender embraces. She was his dream girl.

Jan was equally smitten. She desired a man like Jerry; who was financially secure and respectful. And it was particularly important to her that Jerry got along with his parents because, in her mind, that meant he had the capacity to get along with her own father and that they would become friends. It didn't hurt that Jerry wasn't poor and that he understood the importance of family.

Jerry earned his wealth as a trader at Chicago's commodity exchange. Jan worked at a local department store. She was lucky if she brought home $50,000 a year. Jerry wanted to take care of her; so after living together for a year in Jerry's upscale Lincoln Park home, they decided to marry. Besides, both of them were thirty and they wanted a family.

Prior to the marriage, Jerry sat down with me so I could advise him how to protect his assets and wealth by drawing up and having Jan sign a prenuptial agreement. Jerry said he was sure it would be necessary, but after I shared some horror stories with him, he decided to follow my advice.

At first, Jan was taken aback and reluctant, but she agreed to sign the prenuptial agreement, possessing the same "rosy" outlook that Jerry had. It was merely a formality. They were in it for the long haul.

The wedding came and went and the newlyweds settled into married life, creating an intimate circle of other couples who lived in the neighborhood, many of whom had small children. Most were very close in age.

Jerry and Jan's closest friends were three couples who lived on their block. They frequently met at the local health club or Starbucks on weekends, went out as a group or in pairs, and they vacationed together as well. Individually, the guys played tennis and poker, and the woman enjoyed girls-only activities.

Jerry became especially close to Brian and Lori. Since his typical workday began at 5 a.m., when he traded from home or the Commodity trading floor downtown, when he called it quits in the afternoon, he habitually went to the health club where, more times than not, he met up with Lori. They played tennis and took yoga classes together.

Meanwhile, Jan worked long hours in her retail job, in hopes of being promoted. When she came home after exhausting days, all she wanted was a quick dinner and bed. Due to Jerry's early schedule, he too was in bed by 9 p.m. For six years, this was the routine they settled into as they both pursued their ambitions.

Despite her craving for a promotion and the money and

prestige, Jan was also hoping to get pregnant and become a full-time mother, but they were unsuccessful. Despite two years of trying, the reality of possibly winding up childless weighed heavily on both Jan and Jerry. Depression and disappointment led to troubling changes in Jan's personality. The once-vivacious woman, whose interests knew no bounds, had become a stranger to those passions. She was no longer the fun, vibrant person Jerry married. Jerry began thinking of a life without her.

Brian, Lori's husband, was an optometrist who worked almost every day except Sundays. Lori married Brian because he was a good guy, they had friends in common, and she knew he would be a stable family man who would have a reliable profession to fall back on. Lori supported her husband in every way, and when the children arrived, it was decided that she would quit her job to run the family.

When Brian started his own practice, Lori helped out by scheduling appointments and handling financial matters related to the business. She really enjoyed all of these tasks. Besides, she could bring the kids to the office, which saved them plenty of childcare costs.

In time, Brian's practice prospered and he eventually hired staff to handle Lori's duties. They purchased a home in Lincoln Park and began living a comfortable life. Lori never expected that the man she married would morph into a workaholic, but that's exactly what happened. Lori suggested hiring a part-time doctor so Brian wouldn't feel compelled to work 24/7. She wanted them to spend more time together, but he did not want to give up control.

As the children became more independent, Lori had little to do except make plans with her girlfriends or her mother, to go shopping, or run errands. Having Jerry as her gym friend was a lifesaver, and for a very long time, the two of them maintained a breezy, platonic friendship. But, what started innocently turned into a relationship that began to blossom as they began to confide in and trust each other.

Neither Lori nor Jerry can recall the day their relationship took a turn—perhaps it was the first time Jerry asked Lori for marital advice, a paradoxical thing to do since he knew Lori wasn't too crazy about Jan; putting up with her just because the couples' clique was tight. On the day he turned to Lori to get her perspective and solicit ideas to repair his marriage, things changed. They just didn't know it, yet.

As for Lori, at first she was reluctant to tell Jerry she had married Brian more for security than for love, but once it was out, she couldn't stop. She, too, was lonely and married to an infrequent companion who lacked passion.

Lori told Jerry that she would not have said anything about his marriage, but since he had asked, she would express her opinion: "I think you would be better off divorcing her. Jan suffers from depression and you can't cure her problems." Lori assured Jerry that there was a good woman for him out there, and he realized that her advice was sincere.

It took about two weeks for Jerry to come to peace with the decision to divorce; he made it without further conversations with either woman.

That's where I came into the picture. Jerry called me to discuss his decision. We spent a couple of weeks planning for the divorce, making sure we did what we could to protect his premarital assets. I recommended he close out their joint credit card accounts.

Once all the divorce planning was in place, the divorce papers were served.

Jan may have been depressed, but not so depressed that she couldn't sleuth out one of the best divorce law firms in Chicago. Like a general declaring a call to battle, the legal system began morphing at warp speed. First, the court ordered Jerry to pick up Jan's legal bills. She had wasted no time in giving her attorney the lowdown on his finances, and as her representative, her lawyer encouraged her to go for a huge chunk of Jerry's assets.

Is this usual behavior? Yes! Jan was behaving like the textbook scorned woman who thought she could get revenge by punishing him by getting her hands on as much money as possible. Her attorney stoked the flames of revenge.

Jerry was willing to do whatever it took to free himself. "I'm willing to pay her more money to settle," he confided to me. "Frankly, in the end, it's less expensive than handing you a blank check and suffering through a lengthy battle with no end." I made offers of settlement until her attorneys advised her to settle. Jan got more money than she was legally required to get; yet, she walked away feeling miserable.

While all of this was raging, Lori continued to fantasize about an affair with Jerry. Although she didn't act on her fantasies, the more time they spent together, the deeper the feelings she felt for him. She came to realize that he was the first man she had ever loved, despite the fact that they had not been physically intimate.

Free at last to live his life, Jerry stopped working completely (on my recommendation during the divorce so his income was not an issue during the negotiations). He and Lori spent more and more time with each other.

One day, she volunteered to help Jerry fill out an online dating service profile. They found themselves laughing and joking as she asked him questions posed by the service so he could then decide what to write. Serendipity kicked in. Jerry looked at Lori, and in an instant, he realized that filling out this litany of forms was a useless waste of his time. His dream girl was sitting right in front of him.

Perhaps it was the look on his face that made Lori realize the two of them had moved from friendship to love. They looked at each other in astonishment before Lori left her chair, sat on his lap, and flung her arms around Jerry. The two shared a passionate kiss and before too long they moved to the bedroom where the sex was unparalleled.

Neither felt guilty, nor did either of them deny they felt they were true soul mates—but a large barrier stood in the way of moving forward: Lori was still married. At that moment, she decided to divorce Brian. She wanted to make his life miserable, so that Brian was the one who sought the divorce.

Lori's plan wasn't the most rational one on the planet. At first, Brian joked that Lori's behavior was likely a hormonal issue. Eventually, he reached a point where that explanation didn't hold up and they began arguing. At this point, the children were upset, Lori and Brian were miserable, and the affair between Lori and Jerry continued on. Brian's response to their deteriorating relationship caused him to retreat into his practice, staying such long hours, he often slept on his office couch.

More months dragged by as Jerry's divorce reached a six-month milestone; while Lori and Brian's stalemate showed no sign of being resolved. Lori realized that there was no way to manipulate Brian into asking for a divorce, so she finally asked.

Despite the lousy relationship between Lori and Brian, he was devastated when she said she wanted out of the marriage. Brian blamed himself for being a workaholic. He had always remained faithful to Lori—he loved her and their kids, so when she told him she would be seeking sole custody, he was shocked. But the bonds were irretrievably broken and the Chicago divorce machine ground him up and spit him out.

Brian was in no emotional shape to do more than comply with the court's ruling, which included temporary maintenance and child support. He heard rumors of "another man" in Lori's life, but charged it up to gossip since he continued to blame himself for the breakup.

Brian's self-flagellation came to an immediate halt when he learned that not only were the rumors true, but that the man in question was his best friend, Jerry. He vacillated between shock and anger, wondering why he was so clueless about the affair. Had it gone on for long? He had no idea. Once he passed through all the stages that would have made Elisabeth Kübler-Ross proud, he got pissed off.

He realized that he wanted revenge and would fight Lori in court. It was his turn to make her miserable.

Man Plans; God is in Control

Bill and Kate became lovers while attending graduate school at the University of Chicago. They chose careers in the field of applied economics, with the intention of working for the United States government. According to their peers and professors, the two would have to work hard to be unsuccessful because they were considered to possess two of the best minds the university had seen in recent years. After graduation, both were offered positions at the Chicago offices of the Federal Reserve.

In addition to being intellectually superior, Bill and Kate were sweet, kind, and humble—at least that's how I saw them from the moment I met them when we happened to introduce ourselves as neighbors. We all lived in quaint, spacious, vintage apartments near the campus in Chicago's Hyde Park neighborhood. I moved a few years later, but they remained.

During the summer, Bill and Kate loved to walk to the lakefront and ride their bicycles into Chicago along the Lake Michigan bicycle path. In winter, they enjoyed exploring cute shops in the neighborhood and, on occasion, when I was back in the old neighborhood, I ran into them. Frankly, they seemed more in love than ever and I could see that they remained inseparable. They put me on their wedding invitation list, and I concluded that the ceremony and reception would be as idyllic as they were.

Given their personalities and propensity for planning, I wasn't surprised to learn that the next big step Bill and Kate planned to take was having kids. We laughed when we talked about the approach they were taking to plan for offspring.

"You guys are acting like a couple of economists!" I said.

"You would expect us to act otherwise?" Kate responded with a chuckle.

After a while, things got—well, at least in my eyes—a bit obsessive. This couple planned everything down to the last detail: the size of the house or apartment they would need, the cost of raising one or more children, and then underwriting everything from daycare to college. They even factored in impingements on their income as a direct result of taking time off to attend school and extra-curricular activities.

The couple purchased a book of popular children's names and developed a matrix for room colors based on what today's psychologists recommend in terms of color and shape stimulation during the formative years; and even wound up in a heated discussion about whether to make every aspect of the nursery "green" to show that they were environmentally sensitive.

Bill and Kate's friends, of which I was one, sat back in amazement as the pair never doubted that they would get pregnant despite having started late. Given the degree to which the pregnancy was planned and the overarching precautions she took, it seemed odd that the couple took a pass on pre-screening tests recommended by the OB/GYN given Kate's age.

"What's the matter with you?" I asked

"There's too much chance I could lose the baby or damage the fetus with invasive tests," Kate assured me. "I haven't had a taste of alcohol. I've never eaten so healthfully. And I've never stopped exercising."

All of us figured nothing would go wrong—until we learned that after only five hours of labor, Kate had given birth to a baby with Down's syndrome. Their son would have physical limitations and, even with schooling, doctors said not to expect him to surpass having an IQ equivalent greater than an eight- or nine-year-old.

As Kate held and rocked her baby, tears flowed, but once they dried, Kate the planner emerged from the fog.

"Bill," Kate whispered, "we are going to beat the odds. Our son is going to be the poster child for Down's. He will learn and achieve—go to college and live a normal life."

Perhaps she could will that outcome, friends said. And Bill could only agree; he too was shocked and scared, both for the future and for their relationship.

For the next eight years, Kate dedicated her life to their son and became an expert on the topic of Down's syndrome. Kate quit her job soon after her maternity leave ended, dedicating herself to their son fifteen hours a day. She established hygiene practices he was able to master and she worked with him on learning the alphabet and applied mathematics. Kate read stories to the boy as if a constant spoon-feeding of knowledge would be absorbed and he would, indeed, turn out to be that poster child.

Physically, she never wavered. She put him through a daily regimen of physical activities and therapy. Their son had become Kate's full-time, unpaid occupation.

For eight years, Bill remained a good, faithful husband. He tried to be a good father, but he could never come close to equaling the amount of care and nurturing Kate exhibited. And though Kate remained the love of his life, she was no longer the same woman he had married.

It started routinely. Understandably, after a long day of caring for their child, Kate wanted rest. Sex and companionship ultimately disappeared. In fact, the couple seldom had time for intimacy and made no effort to get away so they could focus on their love for each other. To add insult to injury, when they did have sex, Kate was adamant about using protection. She feared having another special needs child.

Bill wanted more children. He prayed that his Kate—she of the cute smile and contagious personality—would return eventually. But as the saying goes, God laughs while people make plans. Their son died before his ninth birthday.

Bill hoped that once they both got through their mourning, they could resume the loving relationship they had known before they became parents. And at Bill's insistence, they were both tested for genetic abnormalities. He was delighted to find out that their baby's Down's was not the result of chromosomal or other congenital predispositions. Despite what Bill saw as outstanding news, Kate flatly informed him that she never wanted to have a child again.

She saw a psychiatrist who concluded that Kate suffered from such guilt, she could not forgive herself. The beautifully planned life Kate and Bill assumed would be theirs was nothing more than fantasy.

Guilt weighed heavily on Bill, too, but because he was not as obsessive as Kate, he began to get back in touch with his optimistic side. When last I saw him, Bill told me that he confronted Kate, said he not only wanted more children but that he wanted a fresh start, which required a divorce so he could get on with his life.

The toll this catastrophic outcome had on their relationship made me particularly sensitive to what happens when people are incapable of dealing with the curve ball that fate throws at them.

As for Bill and Kate, they still keep in touch. She moved to Washington D.C., where she successfully resuscitated her career; and she has stayed true to her commitment never to marry again. I received an announcement for Bill's upcoming wedding to a nice girl; they are planning for children.

Section II

When You Think of Chicago...

People Get Burned When They Play Games

George is a lover and a player. His weakness for women is only exceeded by his ego. The man has enjoyed the chase for many years, but truth is, he comes overwhelmed with each new romance. Our meetings begin with his telling me about his special, new girlfriend and a video of her undressing.

George loves to fall in love; adores the excitement of seducing a woman until she falls in love with him. He admits to being a sucker for the first soft kiss and physical touching. When asked to describe how he feels when he first touches the skin of a new conquest, he gets downright poetic. In other words, when it comes to falling in love, he never outgrew adolescence.

I find it fascinating that my friend George is such a contradiction. Despite being driven by lust, he is fiercely protective of his business, his home, and his investments. I've helped him with his assets, trusts, and corporate responsibilities; as a numbers man myself, I am impressed by his financial acumen.

His personal life? Not so much. You see, George has already

been married three times and two of them were named Cheryl! You can imagine our crowd's ability to take that happenstance and turn it into a joke or two.

On the plus side of what I like to call George's "Cheryl Binge" is the fact that these divorces have made him something of a master when it comes to personal-asset protection. Circumnavigating three marriages and coming out at the other end not just solvent but comfortable has earned my respect; though as his financial advisor and legal counselor, I like to think I had a part in his fiscal survival. Consequently, whenever George's elevated pulse morphs into signs that marriage number four is in the near future, we start talking prenuptial agreements.

Among the interesting women George met during a recent hunt is Sari. She had all the makings of a rescue queen, including having just come out of a bad, abusive marriage that caused her extreme mental anguish. Her divorce process was equally brutal. Having survived it, she vowed never to marry again.

For a while, she spent evenings home alone, sipping a glass of red wine, lounging in bed, and reading romance novels. Those books helped her escape from reality and they must have also triggered the past because she began recalling dreams she had of happiness and romance—the idyllic match she had assumed was hers when she married her abusive college sweetheart.

Eventually Sari did go out, after a girlfriend refused to stop urging her to skip a night of paperback escapism and re-introduce herself to Chicago's social scene. It was a cold winter's night and the place was crowded because it was Friday and everyone was chilled to the bone and eager to relax after a long work week.

George was there—sitting at a piano bar on Ontario Street. When Sari walked in with her equally compelling girlfriend, he spotted her immediately. It mattered not that her body language screamed "I've lost all hope of ever finding love again."

Sari's friend had picked out a silky blue dress for Sari to wear, with a revealing front slit that enhanced Sari's beautiful sculptured legs and a very sexy neckline to boot. The blue silk scarf she wore completed the outfit; it was more decorative than armor against the frigid temperatures outside.

George immediately decided he would approach Sari before other guys could close in. When Sari's friend received a text from her daughter and stepped outside, he sprang like a jaguar, presenting her with a glass of red wine after taking note of the glass from which she sipped.

Sari was a little flummoxed at first. She couldn't figure out why he had singled her out, but it only took a minute or two before she succumbed to his handsome face and finely tailored suit. He took the girlfriend's seat and, when she protested, he assured Sari that he was just being a placeholder until her friend returned.

When Sari caught a glimpse at his left hand and saw no wedding ring, she took a deep breath.

George knew it would be just a matter of time before the girlfriend reappeared, so he had to move fast. He whispered into Sari's ear that she had beautiful lips and haunting eyes, adding that he was attracted to her.

Sari assumed he was drunk or blind to find her so attractive, but she found his compliments to be overwhelming. It had been so long since someone found her desirable. She soaked up the attention like a sponge. He continued to touch her hand and whisper in her ear. It felt like a giant cliché to realize she felt as though she had become a character in one of her romance novels; as a matter of fact, she felt like Cinderella.

Sari's friend returned after what seemed an eternity and informed Sari that she was having babysitter issues that couldn't be resolved by phone. She had to cut the evening short. "Do you want to come with me?" she asked, eyeing George and wondering how he had moved in so fast.

"I think I'll stay," Sari responded. "I'm just getting to know George. Talk to you tomorrow!" She jumped up and gave her friend a hug good-bye.

Glasses of red wine came and went. One minute it was 9 p.m. and the next it was midnight. She was on Pumpkin Coach time; fascinated, intrigued, and conflicted. Her body wanted to go home with George, but her heart wasn't ready. He insisted on hiring a cab to get her home and promised to call.

And he did. About an hour after the two of them parted.

Over the next two weeks, George smothered her with attention. Sari was caught up in the excitement of this whirlwind romance, feeling more and more like a teenager experiencing sex and romance for the first time. The sex was excellent. George pleased her in every way and she seemed insatiable.

Six months later, George called me to say that he and Sari, were married by the cruise ship captain during an unplanned ceremony off the shore of a Caribbean island on a moonlit night.

My response? "What happened to the dude who could have taught divorced couples a thing or two about hasty marriages and asset protection?"

You know what I'm about to tell you next, right? The honeymoon ended too soon for Sari. After returning home, she began to notices changes in George's behavior. Sex was still very good between them but it was already falling into the categories of routine and boring for George. He had, in the words of the quintessential hunter, bagged his quota. George was being George.

When Sari turned to friends, they all reassured her that no one is capable of remaining affectionate 24/7 forever. "You need to take a breath and give the guy a break."

"But, he's always working late. I swear, I'm starting to think Prince Charming may have found a new princess."

She didn't mean to turn into a suspicious wench, but after all, she did have to check his shirt collars before handing them over to the dry cleaner.

No Sherlock training required: she spotted traces of both lipstick and perfume.

The following week, George told Sari that he had a business meeting to attend that evening. She replied that she would attend a wine tasting with friends. I don't have to tell you that she went to the piano bar, do I? From her vantage point, she recognized George's trademark moves. After all, it hadn't been that long since he had made them on her.

Sari left the bar without being noticed and went home. When George quietly returned at 2 a.m., Sari pretended to be asleep; so he slumbered away that night, feeling smug and excited about his new conquest. The next evening, Sari confronted George. "I thought we had something special; a forever love," she said, sounding very much like a page from the novels she adored. "Who is she?"

George stammered and adverted looking into her eyes. When he realized that the first story he tried was unbelievable, George eventually admitted his guilt to Sari. In a voice so small she was tempted to ask him to speak up—were she not appalled by his answer—he said that the girl was a friend's daughter. And yes, she was nearly half his age, which made it even more exciting.

"You know, I'm not sure getting married was such a great idea," George said, now that the iceberg of lies was starting to melt. But take responsibility? Not exactly. "You pressured me into marrying you.

"Sari, you can leave with the clothes you are wearing now or leave in the morning, it makes no difference to me."

According to those who heard the story later, Sari's rage was white hot and her emotions raced between anger and hatred, but she held back the tears and pretended to acquiesce. She began packing her clothing and informed George that she would sleep in the guest bedroom and then be gone in the morning.

George's mind raced as it did every time he weaseled out of one relationship to move onto the next. He slept the sleep of the not-so-innocent, thinking about the morning when he would be as free as a bird, ready to resume his life exactly where he had left it when he met Sari.

Sari was obviously in no shape to sleep, so she wandered the house a bit and, as if to make her morning departure more real, she put her bag and a few of the personal items she collected when she toured their house for the last time into her car and locked the door.

According to the fire marshal, tests taken at the site the following morning indicated intentional arson originating with what appeared to be a common gasoline canister; the type that most homeowners keep on hand to start their lawnmowers. But Sari targeted everything but the lawn mower, now charred but still recognizable in the rubble.

She had done a thorough job of it, said the police when they called me, because I was identified as George's financial consultant and attorney thanks to Sari's confession. Fortunately, only the house, the furnishings and the car fell victim to her escapade.

George survived the fire and I helped him file criminal charges against her once he completed a monumental recovery and rehab program that left him physically scarred despite plastic surgery. George complained big time when the judge ordered him to pay for her criminal defense attorney. The divorce judge ordered him to pay for her divorce attorney, too.

I'd love to say that George learned the biggest lesson of all from this nightmare experience, during which he nearly lost his life—but frankly, he's back in the game and he's been using the catastrophe as a great way to play the heartstrings of women he meets. The last time we talked, he had just fallen in love with a new, very young woman. Figures.

Is it Better to Divorce Him or Kill Him?

As his new estate-planning attorney, I was asked to update Carl's last will and testament. The guy's an infamous Chicago character with political connections and his house, in an upscale black neighborhood, had the distinction of once being owned by a famous African-American entertainer; so I was curious to see the place.

Carl had been confined to a wheelchair since an assassination attempt cut short his active involvement in several profitable businesses that were jump-started thanks to the aforementioned political connections. Included among Carl's impressive assets was a young trophy wife named Delores.

Upon entering the house, the first thing I noticed was that all of the furnishings were covered in heavy, clear plastic. I was no stranger to plastic-covered seating: back in the 1960s, our mothers were a little bit obsessive about protecting their seating, but I certainly never expected a person with such a high profile to worry about soiling furniture. I mean, the man could afford to buy new furniture as often as he wished.

When I expressed an interest in seeing the house based on its former owner, Carl was happy to give me a tour. Apparently, the tour took longer than he had intended. "I have to apologize for ending the tour," he said after glancing at a clock. "Would you mind if we discuss my will while I have my massage and whirlpool therapy treatments?"

Who was I to say no? He pointed the way to a room off the kitchen that was dominated by a whirlpool so huge, it could compete with any I had seen in health clubs. Beside the pool, a hoist had been installed to lower his crippled body into and out of the water.

I looked around to find a place to sit so I could avoid watching him being undressed. While the hot water splashed around his body and onto the tile floor, we discussed the changes he envisioned for his estate. Because the whirlpool jets were so noisy, we found ourselves shouting at each other!

I took notes, asked questions, and then we agreed to meet again. He needed additional time to determine who he would trust to carry out his final wishes. Carl, it seemed, was not a trusting soul.

You can imagine my shock a few days later when I turned on the TV just as a news anchor was breaking the lead story: a Chicago businessman named Carl had been murdered.

Unaccustomed as I was to having clients die on me this early in a relationship, I wasn't sure what to do; so I waited for more details. It took no time for the second chapter in this Shakespearean play to hit the news: Delores had been charged with his murder. And so was Carl's chauffeur.

Carl was nobody's fool. I knew he intended to disinherit Delores in the event he suffered an untimely death and fortunately, a prenuptial agreement executed before the marriage granted Carl the right to divorce Delores without paying her maintenance. To the best of my knowledge, I don't think Carl told Delores of his plan to change his will.

But, wait! My mind wandered back to our close encounter of the loud kind as Carl and I shouted back and forth over the noisy

Jacuzzi jets. Had she overheard our discussion? Did that set off the firestorm that led to Carl's death?

As it turned out, the chauffeur had a big mouth. And to save his derrière, he told the Chicago police the whole story in lurid detail. A few days after my visit, Carl had the chauffeur drive him around town so he could run errands. When he returned home, he found Delores naked in the whirlpool, sipping a glass of wine. She asked Carl to join her and promised that she would do something special to make him feel good. Things got awkward as the chauffeur assisted Carl into the pool using the hoist; then he left temporarily.

Delores had brought two bottles of wine to the therapy room. She poured wine into Carl's glass and the two of them toasted, drank, and flirted. Somewhere between the third and fourth glasses of wine, the chauffeur returned, put his hands on Carl's shoulders and shoved his head under water. According to the medical examiner's report, the chauffeur's nails had dug into Carl's shoulders as he pushed his boss under the swirling waters.

Delores orchestrated and observed the murder without batting an eyelash, claimed the chauffeur, who kept insisting to the police that it was all her idea. He stated that she continued sipping wine as Carl struggled for his life. Once he stopped struggling, Delores dried off and her lover and she went to a barbeque ribs joint for dinner.

Their alibi? Carl must have had an accident while the two of them were out for dinner and when they returned, they found his body floating face down in the whirlpool.

Delores called the police to report the accident and was able to put on a pretty good act of sounding distressed, but it didn't dawn on either Delores or the chauffeur to come up with a story that made any sense in light of the fact that Carl was wheelchair bound and couldn't get into the tub on his own.

Is it Possible
to Die from Boredom?

Two wealthy students fell in love at the University of Arizona. Townley actually made his fortune while in college by starting a software company that produced a wildly popular mobile phone game. Because he was young and entrepreneurial, all of his wealth was tied up in the goodwill value of his company.

Margaret was born into a wealthy family; so she was, in every sense of the term, a trust fund baby thanks to her father and grandfather. That she happened into a relationship that would keep her in the lifestyle she had grown accustomed to was fortuitous, but there was genuine love between them that led to romance; marriage; and three wonderful, healthy children. A stately house on the side of a mountain, overlooking acres of Arizona wilderness, was icing on the cake. For years, Margaret and Townley enjoyed life in the rich-and-famous lane.

While Townley's talent for innovation had earned him wealth beyond measure, he grew sloppy and stopped keeping up with the technological changes in the software industry. To make things worse, he failed to track the changing tastes of his audience, so his software company was moving at warp speed into oblivion. Filing for bankruptcy was his only solution and the family was forced to sell the Arizona house and move to Oakbrook, Illinois, where Margaret's parents lived.

Margaret's family business remained a hugely prosperous conglomerate of business entities. Margaret was immediately given a high-profile job that provided plenty of income so she could support her husband and kids until he was re-situated. It was a win-win situation all around: Margaret's father always wanted his daughter to learn the business and become his heiress apparent. Now, his dreams were being realized.

Townley quickly became frustrated by his wife's role as family breadwinner and he made no effort to conform to the role of house husband with childcare responsibilities. Since all three children were under the age of ten, Townley was reduced to driving carpools and juggling myriad household responsibilities. Additionally, he wasn't thrilled to be living in such close proximity to his in-laws, who may not have expressed their feelings verbally, but Townley could see it on their faces every time they were together.

When Townley accidentally overheard his father-in-law questioning Margaret about "why she married the loser," he wanted to dig a hole and bury himself. It didn't help that Margaret proved to be a business whiz thanks to her education and the experience she gleaned helping her husband with his software company. She shone when it came to product development, accounting systems, marketing insights, and even IT savvy. To reward her, she was named Chief Operating Officer, given a huge raise, and even a dinner to announce her promotion.

Townley, meanwhile, grew increasingly bored. He no longer had to do the chores he hated because Margaret hired a full-time housekeeper. Feeling dejected and desperate, it wasn't long before his eyes began to wander in a desperate attempt to escape his life.

Townley didn't have to look any further than the carpool to connect with a lonely woman who also felt ignored and unappreciated by her spouse. Both felt alive again as they planned and shared trysts that pumped them both up with excitement and thrills. Because she was so involved in the business, it took a while for rumors to reach Margaret, but denial knows no socio-economic boundaries. She turned a deaf ear to the gossip, but it persisted and she found herself compelled to hire a private investigator to find out whether or not the rumors were true.

After spending very little time on the case, the private investigator found what he was looking for, since neither Townley nor his paramour bothered to take precautions to prevent being caught. After the initial shock, the PI's report enraged Margaret. "That piece of shit husband is having an affair while I work long hours to feed us?" she asked the investigator, who looked sympathetic as he collected his last check. "Why doesn't he appreciate all I've done to support our family?"

Her anger turned to rage. Margaret sought revenge.

And this is when I entered the picture.

Margaret did not want a simple divorce. She wanted to destroy Townley and leave him penniless. She didn't care what impression this would make on the kids because revenge blinded her. Suddenly, she felt relieved that she had lost the battle to her father about his insistence to draw up a prenuptial agreement as a precondition of his approval for the marriage. Margaret's income, assets, and parental gifts were protected and beyond the reach of any divorce court.

Margaret hired me because I have a wicked reputation for being ruthless when it comes to financial dealings. She instructed me to make Townley's life miserable. Every week, we subpoenaed additional documents and then returned them as being incomplete. Every week we came up with accusations of new offenses that Townley was perpetrating. Townley was in court so often, he wished he lived closer to the courthouse.

The depth of the situation grew and, as the other woman

became the centerpiece of our case, her husband left her and a battle for the custody of their children ensued.

But I was focused on my client. Since her father offered the equivalent of an open checkbook, I could muster all of the resources I needed to win this case.

Margaret's custody battle grew so contentious, against my advice, she fought to keep Townley away from their kids, even denying him visitation rights. Because she played the "emotional harm to the children" card, the court ordered Townley, the children, and Margaret to meet with a psychologist before he would be allowed unsupervised visitation.

The long-waged battle took its toll. Townley was denied visitation for almost one year, as we continued to insist on more family counseling sessions. Since we had the money and the wherewithal to keep things going, time droned on.

Influenced by Margaret's stories, that were substantiated by the children, the psychologist was heavily influenced and, erring on the side of caution, her report to the court stated that she believed unsupervised time with their dad would harm the children.

After two years of contentious battling, the stress under which Townley had been living reached a breaking point. The doctors are still not sure if it contributed to Townley being diagnosed with a fast-spreading type of cancer. They urged him to reduce his stress so he could battle the disease to buy as much time as possible.

Townley gave up. He sought to settle all monetary issues remaining in the divorce, requesting only enough money from the remaining marital assets to pay his attorney. By this time, Margaret's anger had become beyond irrational; not to mention the fact that expenses related to her divorce had just surpassed $900,000. She knew the divorce was killing Townley, so she wanted to increase the legal actions.

I know what you're thinking—but it was my job to take care of the legal aspects of my client's charge and not to deliver lectures to her about finding a less expensive way to defuse her hatred. I hoped she would continue seeing the psychologist after things were settled at the final dissolution on December 5th.

Townley was in hospice care and couldn't be at the court-house. He died before Christmas. Margaret told her parents that she received her Christmas present early that year.

What is the Going Price for a Dead Spouse?

I admit it. I am a nag when it comes to lecturing my clients on the benefits of putting together a game plan before they begin the divorce process. Planning will save time, money, and generally secure a better outcome. If they fail to listen, the legal costs increase, which is good from my perspective.

Tommy desired to purge himself from Susie. They were in their late forties and their kids were now in college. The costs of separating caused him to reconsider divorce and seek other forms of redress. His legal practice was both successful and lucrative. If he divorced Susie, he would be forced to pay her maintenance for the rest of her life. Second, Susie—shall we say—became obese. It was difficult to imagine anyone having physical desires for her; so, I can imagine how he felt living with her 24/7.

While Tommy worked out his emotions by pouring himself into his legal practice, Susie maintained her routine: meet friend for coffee at Starbucks, walk the dog, chat up her mom, play cards or mahjong, and then dine alone because Tommy regularly stayed in the city for ball games, dinner with clients, or meet-ups with friends.

Tommy finally admitted to me that he wanted to do more than talk about getting out of the marriage, but of course, the inevitability of Susie being entitled to a considerable share of their joint assets and his future income reared its ugly head. I pushed him to admit that Susie had always been a taker. She never worked or in any way contributed to the household monetarily, but Tommy knew that Illinois divorce law was truly blind. It would favor his wife after so many years of marriage.

When I left Tommy that night, I gave myself a couple of pats on the back for verbally slapping Tommy around until he saw the light. What I didn't know was that rather than starting to get his ducks in a row, he happened upon a Sunday *New York Times* review of a mystery about a husband who terrorized his wife until she committed suicide. A cold chill ran down his spine.

The diabolical plan he began to devise, sadly, made him feel more alive than he had felt in years. Tommy's plan was to make Susie think that her mind was slipping and her memory failing; so he began taking Susie's wallet out of her purse and stashing it in the kitchen junk drawer. He transferred her house keys from her purse to her coat pocket. Tommy's days and nights were so filled with devising fantastical schemes that he began to forget things to the chagrin and dismay of his work staff, but he felt that his mission justified a little absentmindedness.

The stunts grew more creative. He mixed up the medicines in her pill. He took her house keys and put them in the front door lock, as if she forgot to remove the key when entering the house. His favorite was when he changed the date on her phone; it caused her to miss every appointment. He admonished himself as juvenile, petty, and petulant, but it became an obsession he couldn't stop.

At the time, I knew nothing about his scheme. I figured that the reason we no longer spent time together was that he wanted to spare me the details and suffer in private. Little did I know.

Assuming she was losing her mind, Susie literally took to her bed, getting up only to replenish groceries. She stopped going to Starbucks, meeting with friends, and playing cards. This behavior filled Tommy with glee since he was succeeding. His piece de resistance was shuffling the speed dial codes on her phone and then changing the dates and times of doctor's appointments and the few activities in which she was still engaged. Suspecting dementia, Susie was in panic mode 24/7. The coup de grace? Susie filled her car with gas every Wednesday afternoon. Late that night, Tommy siphoned the gas from the tank so when she tried to start the car the next morning, the gas gauge read empty.

A mile from the house, in an intersection, Susie telephoned Tommy, broke down, and cried so uncontrollably Tommy couldn't understand a word she was saying. Of course, he had been waiting for this call; which is why, out of the blue, he asked his office staff to put through any calls from his wife despite a longstanding policy: "If my wife calls, take a message." He felt obliged to return home to experience his handiwork, pretend to be the concerned caring husband. He wore a huge grin all the way home.

Pretending to be concerned, Tommy asked Susie to describe what was going on. She confided that she was losing her memory and began stating all of the reasons she had reached that conclusion. Tommy did the best he could to appear sympathetic as suggested she might want to get a new psychiatrist—obviously the one she was using wasn't helping. He calmly suggested she might need Prozac or another antidepressant.

Susie agreed to find another shrink and take whatever drugs he or she prescribed. This meant that Tommy was going to have to up the ante in terms of his little tricks because if he could prove to the courts that even on meds she remained a danger to herself or others, his ultimate dream—of seeing her on visitation days at a local mental health facility—had moved from the realm of possibility to "Hell, yes! I can get her committed!"

The dirty tricks kept up until the day she grew so confused, a hospital called to inform Tommy that Susie's stomach was being pumped after paramedics found her in a stupor after taking several of her pills because she couldn't recall whether or not she had taken her daily dose. She recovered and was sent home. Tommy was running out of patience but he smelled victory.

He didn't have to wait much longer. A couple of weeks later, Tommy received a telephone call from the Deerfield police. His wife had stopped the car on an overpass, got out, left the car running, climbed over the railing, and jumped to her death onto the highway below.

Tommy pretended to be distraught, but within months of finishing his period of "mourning," Tommy was actively dating and enjoying life.

It took months for Tommy to confide the story of his madness campaign to me. I didn't believe a word of it. But he does know that attorneys and clergy are sworn to silence.

Section III

The Children

Words Can Scar
Your Children Forever

I'm fairly active in the operation of my synagogue. I attend services fairly regularly and I'm always eager to meet new attendees so I can encourage their active future participation in our programs and services. On one particularly gloomy evening, I arrived just as the traditional evening prayer was beginning; that's when I noticed Devora. She was saying the mourner's prayer known as The Kaddish. Tears dripped down her cheeks as she said the words ever so slowly.

Every Jew has their own way of mourning the dead. Devora seemed to be so immersed in her grief, I doubt she noticed me taking a seat near her. At the end of the short service, I turned to her, introduced myself, and offered my condolences on the loss of her loved one.

"My husband," she said tersely. "And it was my entire fault," she added, tears streaming down her cheeks from bright-red eyes. I assumed that Devora had been devastated by losing a part of her life when he died. It was easy to engage her. She wanted to talk with someone and, in this case, I had inquired. I felt comfortable asking about the circumstances surrounding his demise.

"Jacob and I were married for a number of years," she confided. "Most of them the best years of my life. I truly believed that we were and will always and forever remain soul mates, but despite the fact that we loved each other, we fought and bickered continually. We couldn't stay married."

In my job, of course, I am used to hearing these words. I could almost predict her next sentence: "We eventually divorced, and believe me, I made him pay for divorcing me. I even made the children hate him. I told the kids terrible stories about him to pollute their minds."

I wish I could say this was the first time I had heard someone utter these words; but in fact, I might even have predicted them, too.

"He died yesterday. He was buried at Shalom Cemetery. There must have been a hundred friends and co-workers at the grave site; despite the fact it was a windy, sunless, cold, late-October day. Dead brown leaves flew over the freshly dug pile of dirt as the plain, wooden coffin was lowered into the ground. The Rabbi described him as a 'lonely, troubled man who loved his children who disowned him. He valued his friends and was a good man, but it was the loss of family that broke his heart and shortened his life.'"

I thought Devora was very emotional for a woman who obviously didn't want to stay married to her husband; as she continued to describe the setting, I couldn't help but wonder why she shed so many tears. "A dozen chairs were set up for family members to sit on. The only living family member was his mother. The nonfamily members stood.

"After the service ended and friends and family shoveled dirt over the casket, as a final sign of respect, it hit me. I will never be able to apologize to Jacob for what I had done." What she said next saddened me. "Because of me, my kids disowned Jacob's mother, their grandmother; so you can you imagine the courage it took for me to turn to her at the grave site, take her hand, and kiss her, hoping that she would forgive me for being so evil."

Since the usual post-burial ritual included a get-together for friends and relatives to mark the start of the official mourning period called sitting Shiva, her former mother-in-law had invited mourners to her condo for a subdued, modest, one-night reception in her tiny place.

The fact that her only grandchildren were missing at both the funeral and the gathering spoke volumes about the depth of Devora's horrific behavior, made even more painful by the fact that when Devora asked the kids to attend their dad's funeral, they simply refused. "I told them, 'he was your father and he loved you very much.'" But using the words Devora had so carefully selected when she poisoned their minds years ago, both children replied, "He never loved anyone but himself."

Sitting in the synagogue beside Devora was a sobering experience for me. I listen to this kind of stuff every day when counseling my clients—but her story put a face on the amount of destruction one person is capable of doing as a result of anger so profound she resorted to poisoning the minds of her kids.

It was too little, too late. Guilt and grief at the news of Jacob's death was so profound, Devora picked up the phone, called the kids and begged them to attend his funeral. "No matter how much I argued with the children that their father was a good, loving husband and father, my words fell on deaf ears. So, I attended the funeral alone, as my children went on with their day without a second thought that their father was being buried."

Devora's parting words to me were, "I hope that Jacob will find it in his heart to forgive me and the children." That's the last time I ever saw her.

I'll Make His Life Such a Living Hell, He Will Wish He Was Dead

Part 1

Carol, recently divorced, sat with her children at my home, enjoying dinner with my family on a warm spring evening. She lamented the fact that her children had been abandoned by their father. "Mark, my ex, moved out of state because he hated his children," she said without emotion, as dinner dishes were being cleared.

Do I bring my business home and entertain clients? Occasionally, but in this instance, Carol and her kids were invited to dinner because my kids went to school with hers and they had become friends. It became evident that Carol had been unable to move on with her life after her divorce because the topic remained the focus of her conversation throughout the meal. When the kids went to the basement to play, we hoped Carol might have exhausted the topic, but the single mother of three was just getting started.

Carol, it seems, could have been the poster child for *parental alienation syndrome*, as once the children were out of earshot, she launched into a tale that, if half true, was enough to jar our sensibilities. She met Mark and became his "original other women" when the two fell in love—he was a married man at the time. The passion of the affair led Mark to leave his wife and two children. Now married for fifteen years, Carol learned that he had cheated on her with someone else.

"I gave that son of a bitch beautiful children," she said as she calmly described a revenge plan that would be a great script on any soap operas. "I learned about his affair through friends," she said. After going through recent credit card statements, more nails were put into Mark's virtual coffin.

At first, Carol didn't confront Mark. Instead, she thought about how to maximize his pain the most; she was aided and abetted by a local news story profiling the verdict in a child molestation case that was receiving lots of media coverage. "He did unspeakable things to our daughter," Carol said when she called the police the following day and accused him of fondling their three-year-old.

Can you picture my expression as this story effortlessly flowed past Carol's lips? She was actually gloating when she talked about painstakingly rehearsing her child and giving her daughter rewards for repeating back what her mother told her to say. The little girl had even been coached to point to her panties when telling the story.

The police hauled Mark off in handcuffs, during the day when all of the neighbors were home to witness him being slowly walked into the police car, as news cameras filmed the event for the evening news. Carol hired the most expensive divorce lawyer in town. (Forgive me for thinking that I had dodged a bullet because I didn't know Carol at the time. I might have been her choice.)

That stated, when it came to Bad Ass Chicago Divorce Attorneys, she went for a barracuda firm where all of the lawyers had reputations for being assholes without moral compasses who were willing to do what it took to bring a client's spouse to their knees and, in the process, strip them of their reputations and assets.

"I told them, I want to destroy him," Carol said. "That it wasn't about winning. It was about scorn. I want him to know and feel what it looks like."

Part 2

Mark was arraigned after twelve hours in the holding tank. The judge permitted Mark to post bail on the condition that he surrender his passport and that he agreed to not contact his children without a court order. To pay the bail tab, Mark's parents used their home as collateral so Mark could be released from the Cook County Jail. Carol, meanwhile, with faux outrage and disappointment, continued her campaign by calling Mark at his parent's home where he was staying.

"I told him that maybe I had been too quick to accuse him, but that since things hadn't been right between us for a long time, perhaps it was just as well that the situation had come to a head," she said, taking a cookie from the plate on our coffee table. "I loved taunting him; so I added that since they had been best of friends, perhaps we might want to settle things without spending every penny we had on attorneys."

I could see what was coming. The urge to grab her by her sweater collar and throw her out was strong, but I was both riveted by the biggest, most spiteful story I had ever heard and my desire to see how it ended.

The spider was about to set another trap, as Carol arranged with Mark to iron out a divorce settlement at their home around 9 p.m. on a weekend night; the youngest was in bed and the others were at sleepovers. Still in shock since his release from jail, Mark hoped they could be civil despite his well-placed anger; so he was taken aback when Carol opened the door dressed in a revealing outfit and greeted him with a kiss that barely touched his cheek, but she held it long enough to give him a whiff of fragrance that always melted him in the past.

"I invited Mark to sit on the couch. At first, our conversation revolved around the children and financial issues," she said. Carol continued to insist that she wanted a friendly, civil divorce, and her behavior was such that he was lulled into a state of hope. "Imagine his expression when I made some moves on him by telling him that I missed the sex we enjoyed throughout most of our marriage. Honestly, he was like a sheep being led to slaughter when I pulled no punches about how I wanted things to be rough so I could mentally break our ties."

The urge to throttle Carol had grown strong. But I was too fascinated to tell her to stop.

Part 3

After Carol had at last blessedly left with her cranky kids in tow, I felt compelled to jot down in my journal the details of her story thus far. Because while she wasn't a client, she qualified for my journal simply by taking her place among the most despicable women I've met when it comes to divorce revenge-style. I was so sorry for Mark and their children that I couldn't sleep. As I jotted down notes, I tried to ignore the mental picture of her seduction, but had no luck.

This faux seduction was the latest in Carol's diabolical plans for manipulating a proper (in her eyes) divorce settlement. She turned on the steam. Alternately bending over to reveal the barely-there lingerie she wore, interjecting double-entendres into the conversation at strategic points, and employing the occasional stroke of his leg to ram home a point, she could see that her understanding of Mark's hot buttons remained as she remembered them.

But it was her mention of a theme that was new to her vocabulary—rough sex—that pushed him over the top. He lunged and the two fell to the floor in a hot and heavy make-out session that wasn't so much seductive as it was sophomoric in light of their adversarial relationship. Saturated in lust, he forced Carol to get on her knees, ripping off the thong she wore. He didn't bother to take off his pants. Using one hand, he managed to free his penis and penetrate her.

At this point in the retelling of the story, I honestly remember avoiding Carol's eyes. I hardly knew her but she was sitting in my home offering her version of *Fifty Shades of Grey* with a big helping of black. I recall trying to find a place on the floor on which to concentrate as my brain, clever as it is, couldn't come up with a way to extricate myself from her company. Like a captive prisoner, there I sat.

I'll spare you the details. Let's just say that when they were done, she sent Mark off, promising that they would resume the divorce negotiation at a later time. He left the house with a big grin on his face. Carol watched Mark pull out of the driveway, checking her watch to figure out how far he had driven before she straightened herself up and called the police.

I can't swear to it, but I'm pretty sure that my eyes were the size of volcano craters as she described how she cried and pleaded while handing over her torn thong, answered questions, had her bloody knees photographed and changed into sweats for the drive to the hospital where a rape kit confirmed her story. The police picked Mark up in the middle of the night.

"The detective assigned to my case said that Mark went ballistic when he tried to tell the police officer that the sex was consensual and all my idea. Mark even pleaded with them that I wanted it rough and he simply complied with my wishes. I was quite happy with my performance—and deserve an Oscar," she added.

The living hell Carol had promised to rain down on Mark was complete. His reputation for being a charitable community leader, good father and husband crashed and burned once local newspapers picked up the story of his arrest after he was arraigned and charged with both rape and child abuse This time around, bail was denied.

Carol had Mark where she wanted him. Her attorney swooped in and told Mark that if he agreed to her divorce settlement terms and signed the papers he brought to the jail with him, Carol would drop the rape and molestation charges. And, that's what happened. Mark was forced to serve three years' probation. With the court's permission, he moved out of state, but his life was never the same. He now was registered as a sex offender living in fear that everyone he met would see his scarlet mark.

I was so happy to slam that door after finally getting her out our front door that I would have done a happy dance were I prone to such behavior. I needed a shower.

The urge to write Mark a letter was strong, but considering the wrath Carol might rain down on me, I dismissed the thought, deciding instead to declare a moratorium on inviting over kids' parents for dinner.

Her Lost Children

Melissa is the new greeter at my health club, a position that, until she joined the staff, had always been a revolving door of new employees. She also happens to be the daughter of my good friend Gary who, as fate would have it, had his own divorce horror stories with his ex-wife Michelle.

I knew there were always problems with the marriage, ranging from differing child-rearing styles, to lack of affection, and Michelle's need to control everything. Michelle gave in to her kids' whims. Gary was the quintessential wait-until-your-father-gets-home guy. He was the bad guy in the relationship, the enforcer of punishment. Over time, it was clear to those who knew them that Michelle could not share the love of her children with Gary. She needed the children completely dependent on her.

The situation with Gary's parents bordered on toxic. Michelle was critical of Gary's parents in public and in front of their children. The situation was palpable at family get-togethers; so over the years, Gary's family found excuses to stay away from Gary and his wife. Gary craved for the family ties where the cousins could become best friends.

When Gary confided in me that the situation was even worse than I imagined—that Michelle had become so dominating when it came to the kids and their possessions—I tried to decide whether I should put on my lawyer-only hat, my friend-only hat, or wear both of them. As things progressed, it became the latter as Michelle's addiction to credit card spending threatened to bankrupt them. Gary suffered ten years in this loveless marriage and then, when the last child was in high school, he filed for divorce. The divorce was bloodier than most.

Like most battered people, Gary wanted out so badly, he took the easy way out. When Michelle uttered her proclamation that "if you are Gary's friend, you are my enemy," the caveat extended to the kids, and in my experience, children raised in this type of hostile environment always acquiesce to the more dominant parent. Gary was officially persona non grata.

Because he was finally free of her, Gary encouraged his family to try and renew their relationship with his children and they made a good effort, sending dinner invitations, birthday cards, notes from cousins, and invitations to family gatherings like weddings—but the kids had been so manipulated for so many years, that they may still have remained small children in terms of the control Michelle had on them. They didn't respond; so after years of trying, Gary's family gave up.

When Gary and I ran into each other last year at the health club, where his daughter Melissa still works, he told me that Michelle had died, an unexpected turn of events. "My children haven't done well," he confided. Both kids have dead-end jobs, they are unable to maintain relationships, and exist in the fantasy of Internet games.

Never shy about playing matchmaker, I decided that maybe the time had come to mediate a relationship between Gary and his kids. I approached Melissa at the club, extended my condolences on the loss of her mother, and suggested that this might be a good time to heal the old wounds—if not with their father at least with his family. She said she would think about it, but my gut says, "Not gonna happen."

Sometimes even a skilled mediator can read the signs and must give up on further meddling. Every time I see Gary, it breaks my heart, knowing he loves his children, desires to help them—and yet they are unattainable.

These Kids Don't Need a Father

When I first met Barbara, I found it hard to believe my bad luck. I had just come off a horrific experience with the aforementioned Carol when her doppelganger came into my life. The woman manipulated her children like puppets and treated them like pawns. Only Carol was capable of turning in a more convincing performance of the beleaguered wife. There are cases where you hate your client and want to charge extra because of the aggravation factor.

I found out that it took next to nothing to turn Barbara into a sprinkler head, but the faux tears she put on display when the kids were around did nothing more than upset them so much, they stopped asking her why she was crying.

Like Carol, Barbara had her message to the kids down pat: "Your father refuses to give us any money so I'm not sure whether or not I can put food on the table this weekend."

When the "we're going to starve" theme grew thin, Barbara moved onto the company the kid's father kept. "I figured out why we're not getting money for food," she nodded. "He's spending it all on his whores."

Next up came a threat that surpassed the others: "I can't make the mortgage payment. I'm afraid that we're going to be thrown onto the street and the sheriff will take away the dog." The youngest had bed-wetting issues caused by her mastery at manipulating her children's fears and insecurities.

I knew the truth, of course, because I was instrumental in making sure Perry paid his court-ordered support every month like clockwork through the State of Illinois' child support division's payment unit. As a matter of fact, the money wound up in Barbara's bank account as automatic deposits, so she didn't even have to drive to the bank to cash a check.

Frankly, I wanted to say something but it was neither my place to inform the kids that Barbara was full of crap nor could I address this horrific situation properly due to privileged conversations. As Barbara's attorney of record, I could do little more than hope and pray that she did something so awful, Perry would get the kids.

I wish I could take credit for the circumstances that pushed this situation to the brink, but it all goes to Commonwealth Edison. It was winter. Chicago. And suddenly, there was no power. "He's trying to kill us," Barbara told the children. "Your father didn't pay the electricity bill. Now, all of our food is going to spoil." To inject credibility, she claimed that her cell phone was dead; so she drove the kids to a friend's house, burst into the front door, and hysterically claimed that she needed to use her phone to call Perry.

No *Hamlet* soliloquy could have been delivered more convincingly and at a pitch that could be heard throughout the house. Barbara refused to remove her coat, muffler, boots, hat, earmuffs. Melting snow dripped on the kitchen floor while she dialed Perry's number and began to loudly rail at him over a wide assortment of power-related crises that she and the kids were experiencing at the moment. Obviously, a line in the snow had been drawn.

Perry got me on speed dial after he called the power company to learn that the bill had been paid and the outage was caused by cable repairs. "Didn't your wife receive the postcard and phone call explaining that the power would be out for several hours this afternoon?"

Perry's attorney petitioned the court for an emergency hearing requesting a change in custody of the children. The motion cited parental alienation and the spouse's mental health. The judge ordered that all parties attend psychological counseling and therapy. I have only Perry's word to describe what went on during those therapy sessions, but things were grim as Barbara pulled out all stops to malign her husband. The kids had been thoroughly brainwashed—they didn't want any part of their father at this point.

The judge, after reading the therapist's report, stated, "In all of my years on the bench, I've never seen a case of such extreme alienation between father and son." The judge, to verify the therapist's finding met with the children in the judge's chambers without attorneys or a court reporter. Afterwards the judge wondered if these children could ever be rehabilitated, even with the best child therapist's efforts. How bad were the son's accusations? Name a topic and Barbara had covered it: his father had sex with men, women, and prostitutes and refused to give his mother money so they could eat and keep the heat turned on in the winter months.

When the judge handed down her ruling, she gave Barbara the verdict she deserved, railing about the amount of intentional distress and harm that had been caused by lies, exaggerations, and other manipulative behaviors. "Nothing can repair the damage you have caused your children," she told Barbara. But the judge's hands were tied in terms of her ruling. The children stayed with Barbara and everyone received court-ordered mandates to stay in therapy.

Perry didn't get custody, and was only permitted visitation in the presence of the therapist. Perry conducted himself as a gentleman though clearly disappointed, when the inevitable was announced. It took years before he started dating again because his fear of falling in love with another woman like Barbara was profound. Thanks to a skilled therapist he resigned himself to move on. I'm happy to say that, armed with his newfound self-awareness, he is happily remarried to a woman who is the polar opposite of Barbara; and he has two more children.

Does he miss his older kids and wish he had a relationship with them? Of course. Perry is resolved to keep the door open in his life and in his heart, should they ever decide to re-establish a relationship with him. The children were the victims; they continued their lives without a male father figure who would express love and mentoring.

Some Pictures are Priceless

Joyce was going through a contentious divorce and planned to use her twelve-year-old daughter as a pawn to obtain evidence against her husband, Ted.

"Ari, the next time you visit your father, I want you to ask to borrow his smart phone," she instructed. "Tell your father that you want to play games on it—if he should ask. Then check out the photos and call me."

Eager to follow her mother's directive, Ari reviewed her dad's saved photos and found nude pictures of his current girlfriend. Following her mother's instructions, Ari forwarded them to mother's phone. It took Joyce just minutes to send the photos to everyone she knew, even posting them on Ted's Facebook page so his family and friends could view the new love of Ted's life. The pictures left nothing to the imagination and quickly went viral until they were pulled for being obscene.

Joyce next took the photos to court and used them to claim that Ari's father wasn't a good candidate for unsupervised visits with the twelve-year-old. "Your honor, who knows what he could expose my daughter to in light of the fact that he keeps these crass photos on his phone for anyone to see?" Joyce fleshed out her appeal by insisting that these weren't the only photos of nude women he carried on his smart phone. "He's always letting Ari use his phone," she pleaded. "She's young and impressionable and I just don't want her being exposed to any more smut that she has already been privy to," she concluded.

Ted's attorney prepared his client for the worst. "Ted, how can you be so f—in stupid?" he asked.

Ted tried to explain, but his attorney just dismissed him and scared Ted, telling him that he could lose his visitation rights as a result of being so careless.

Ted was forced to face his worst nightmare. He was lectured by the judge about his lack of concern for his daughter's welfare and he immediately suspended Ted's unsupervised visitation rights until he could prove that he had received counseling and completed a sex therapy program.

Ari wasn't called to the stand, and while the judge suspected that Joyce had played a part in this photo drama, nothing could be proven. Ted followed every instruction the judge gave, to the letter of the law, and when he hired me to represent him the next time around, he said he felt he had learned his lesson.

As we approached the courtroom to have Ted's parental visitation rights restored, I put out my hand. "Hand it over," I said.

"What?"

"Your phone. Now." I checked it out, and finding nothing riskier than a couple of cat photos he had put on his phone. I checked his texts too and knew that if the judge inspected the phone he would pass the test. I handed it back to him.

Love the Internet

"Mommy, there are police cars in the driveway and their lights are flashing," ten-year-old Johnny informed his mother. In fact, there were eight police officers getting out of squad cars and a couple of cars marked FBI. Such a huge presence had attracted quite a crowd of neighbors, all eager to catch a glimpse of whatever untoward was going on at Johnny's house.

As the authorities pounded on the front door, Judy ordered her son to his room and then opened the door. A man in a suit held up an official-looking document and announced that a search warrant was being served that permitted this gaggle of officials to enter the residence. Judy was asked to sign a form and with that, in swept the law enforcement officers.

Despite being asked to go to his room, Johnny was too frightened to leave his mother's side. The two watched, wide-eyed, as the team swept through rooms and filled black bags with property and papers. Her mind raced as she attempted to sort out her confusion while comforting her child as one-by-one, bags were marked and tossed into a marked police van.

"Mommy—that's my computer!" Johnny yelled, but it was too late. It was stowed in the vehicle. A detective who identified himself as being the lead investigator asked Judy if he could have a moment in private. It was all she could do to get Johnny to sit on the couch as she led the officer to the dining room, where Johnny could keep his eyes on his mother.

"Ma'am, do you know your husband's whereabouts?"

"What's this all about?" she asked. "I need an explanation."

"I'm sorry, but I have to talk to your husband—do you know where he is?"

"Jeffrey's at work," she responded. "That computer has my children's homework in it. Can I get it back this evening?" she asked.

"I'm sorry. I'll return the computer and other personal property as soon as our experts analyze the data. It may take several weeks," he added, turning without another word and walking out the door toward his vehicle.

In a matter of minutes, the driveway was completely empty.

Judy soon learned that Jeffrey watched child porn on the Internet and had agreed to meet a fourteen-year-old girl. In fact, she was actually a fifty-year-old male cop conducting a sting operation aimed at catching child predators. Judy settled into a numb state.

Word spread fast in Judy's small community. After the evidence-gathering visit, the children were bombarded with insults and teased at school; this nightmare didn't let up for months. Not a day passed that a reporter or nosy neighbor didn't ask questions. Judy and the kids wanted to hide, but there was nowhere to go to hide.

Jeff was extradited to California for his trial. Judy and the children stayed in Chicago. She demanded a divorce, but since Jeff was in jail awaiting trial, the divorce process was stalled. No criminal court would allow him to fly to Chicago to participate in a civil court divorce matter.

Given the circumstances, Jeff had no financial means to pay for his criminal legal defense nor did he have any source of income as Judy was smart enough to turn to me for help to make sure that any marital monies were frozen and couldn't be used for his defense.

I recall Judy's words to me were some version of "He can rot in hell."

But as easy as it was in the heat of the moment to secure those assets, I had to prepare Judy for possibilities that included these potential scenarios: the divorce court could order Judy to pay support to Jeffrey. She could also be ordered to pay his criminal legal fees. Further, there was a chance she might be told to pay him maintenance, even if he was convicted.

Judy knew that her earnings were insufficient to support the house and the children, but she did not want to be married to a pervert for the next fifteen years, either. After lots of discussion, Judy agreed that her best recourse would be to divorce Jeffrey and pay him a financial settlement out of the family savings he had hoped to use to support her family. He, of course, used the settlement to pay his criminal legal fees.

To this day, Judy and the kids are still haunted by the memory of the day when the house was raided. I have counseled her to move on and recommended support groups. I have also recommended that she move and start a fresh life somewhere else. But, how can I understand how deeply that experience impacted her? Still incapable of trusting another man, she shies away from dating.

Section IV

Money is the Root of Evil and Lousy Divorces

Honey, Where's the Money?

Cathy was married to Ralph for years.
Now she's in her mid-fifties. Having been a stay-at-home mom for most of those years, she felt financially insecure, but when the rug was pulled out from under her upon learning that Ralph had been unfaithful, she worried that if he could hide another relationship from her, had he been honest about their finances?

Cathy went from being a trusting, loyal wife to a woman who feared for her future. She did what many women in her position do: she decided not to acknowledge the fact that she knew of her husband's dalliances. She was hoping that he change, i.e., grow up and be a loving, faithful husband again.

What was behind this willingness to put up with being humiliated? She feared being left alone and without a penny to her name.

Needing support, Cathy disclosed Ralph's infidelities to her closest friends and the news caused an avalanche of feedback. Friends insisted on telling her stories of husbands who socked away hundreds of thousands of dollars that their wives never knew about. When she thanked them for their insight, she left the sarcasm out of her tone.

Cathy's imagination went wild. She began to fantasize. "Maybe the son of a bitch has been socking away money all these years," she found herself muttering as she attacked a roasting pan with a steel pad. "But perhaps my friends have done me a favor," she concluded. By the time the pan was spotlessly shining, Cathy had decided to seek a divorce. The solution became as clear as day.

"I want to be able to control some finances," she told me when we discussed her desire to get a divorce from Ralph. "At least I'll stand a chance to salvage something if the court supervises the allocation of assets." She confided that the moment she started to take some financial control, she felt she had regained the self-respect she had lost.

The process of peeking into other people's financial lives gets to be routine after a while—especially if you work as many cases as I do that reveal the creative approaches married people take once they no longer feel committed to their marriages.

Ralph was a salaried employee at a large, publicly held corporation. He participated in an employer-sponsored 401(k) retirement plan. The couple's marital assets consisted of a house with some equity, stocks, a small amount of 401(k) savings, and a little cash.

I turned one of my paralegals—I like to call her Sherlock because she has a great nose for hidden assets--loose but she wasn't able to find any hidden assets. When I reported back to Cathy and said there were no hidden monies, she refused to believe it. Her friends had done a great job of brainwashing her. At that point, I had no choice but to satisfy my client and use my forensic accounting skills to delve deeper.

Where to start? Over time, I've come to look at income tax returns as puzzles waiting to be solved, but I also faced a dilemma: it can be expensive to conduct a detailed financial forensic analysis—and I rarely recommend them when the case is a small one. But I felt loyal to Cathy, knowing she was pinning her hopes on a Perry Mason moment, where her husband jumps up and fully confesses to his sins. I would discount my fees a bit to help her out.

"The facts will speak for themselves. If there is something to find, I'll tell you. And if there is nothing, I'll tell you that too—but you've got to promise me that if I don't find anything, you'll let this go." I had no way of knowing if Cathy could honor such a promise, but I hoped she would.

I buried myself in my home office with five years' worth of income tax returns and bank records. Not quite a James Patterson-read, but in my line of work, there's lots to be found in between those carefully drawn lines on those iconic IRS forms when matched with bank records.

Nothing. Just as I suspected. Thankfully, I was able to convince Cathy that if she kept on with this obsession, not only would she wind up giving me half of her assets to go on more wild goose chases, but she was going to be really mad at herself down the road when she looked back and realized how she had squandered her money.

"Okay, no Perry Mason moment for me," she said laughing when I brought back all of those old returns and handed her my bill. I'm delighted to report that she accepted the fact that there were no hidden assets and that she could move ahead with her divorce settlement discussions.

Sometimes, He is Not a Prize Worth Having

My firm advertises my forensic accounting services on the Internet, including on social media sites; thus I receive telephone calls from numerous individuals who are in divorce proceedings or contemplating divorce and they're on high alert about financial shenanigans.

Many of the calls are from wealthy women who married men who weren't financially secure—which is the situation with Cindy, a successful attorney earning a substantial annual income as a partner in a national law firm. Partners at her firm generally work between sixty and seventy hours a week. (I'd mention her hourly billable rate, but any dislike you may have toward the legal profession could be exacerbated if I did.)

Not only is Cindy wealthy but she's a Catholic who grew up with "Midwest values" (her term, not mine). You know the type: she achieved academic recognition in college and at the University of Chicago Law School and she wasn't surprised when offered a six-figure associate's salary right out of law school. Through hard work and perseverance, she achieved a dream when she became a partner at a prestigious law firm.

But given her aforementioned self-descriptor as a woman with Midwest and Catholic values, I wasn't surprised to learn that Cindy wanted it all, including having a family, but when I first met her, motherhood remained elusive, despite the fact that she had several relationships as she climbed the ladder to success.

I know what you're thinking, because I thought this too: How does a woman find what she wants when the men she encounters aren't willing to play second fiddle to her career ambitions? Cindy worked late into the night and on weekends, since life as a litigating attorney is dictated by trial dates, emergency motions, and hearings.

On the bright side, all of this work and success meant that Cindy amassed wealth that allowed her to live large. But none of it made up for the fact that Cindy's younger sister had kids; and at times, she admitted to being jealous, wishing she too had a husband and children. She feared she might not have either—until her metaphorical biological clock went off while attending a friend's Super Bowl party where she met Mike.

Mike had been invited by business partners and didn't know a soul, but he didn't much care about that once he met Cindy, the most beautiful woman in the room in his eyes. Mike recalls that his brain completely disengaged when he introduced himself and he began uttering one stupid thing after another. She found him silly and charming; the two of them spent the evening together.

After several drinks, Cindy and Mike relaxed. Mike mentioned owning a construction company. He told Cindy that he had been married and had two children. Cindy could see that Mike was a funny guy and during their conversation, she learned he was Catholic. Wow. Good-looking. Sexy. Straight. Even a business owner. He hit all of her hot buttons.

The two dated for three intense months. Cindy was in heaven. She invited Mike to move into her house so they could spend more time together. Within a year they were married in a church service, though it wasn't the Catholic service she would have preferred since he had been married before.

Mike and Cindy made a cute couple. They shared household chores and Mike was happy to handle their finances. He took over managing investments and Cindy trustingly provided Mike with access to all of her financial accounts. Mike was her soul mate, she thought, and he would be the father of her kids, so why not trust him with her financial matters? Cindy loved having Mike's children at their home, spoiling them with love and attention as she continued to hope that she would give them a brother or sister sooner rather than later.

You know what's coming next, right? Mike's kids were fun as she played the spoiling step-mom every other weekend but they were not a substitute for the child she wanted in her womb. Because she had targeted Mike as "Baby Daddy" material, she even started to resent him for not doing his manly duty and getting her pregnant.

It got worse when Cindy found the financial statements. Apparently, Mike's skills as a contractor did not extend to wisdom on the stock market. Plenty of damage had been done by the time Cindy came to me for help. On top of everything else that was impacting their relationship, Mike's business had failed.

"I allowed him to do as he wanted with our finances and didn't pay attention," she admitted. Now, in addition to feeling foolish, angry, and hurt, she was worried about being broke as well. She asked me to investigate her finances and trace where her monies went and how they had been spent.

After I completed my forensic investigation, I had to inform Cindy that Mike not only mismanaged their investments but swindled money that appeared to have been funneled into his construction business. Feeling that she wouldn't bother to check her accounts—she hadn't for years—he simply went ahead and helped himself to cash from her bank accounts.

I had to tell Cindy that she would never recover the monies he had taken because she had signed numerous documents giving him access to her accounts. I wanted to ask Cindy why she never had Mike investigated before she married him, if only to make sure he was who he seemed to be. When I did some digging into his past, I learned that he was a repeat offender: a previous business failure was funded by his first wife's money.

The psychological damage that Mike caused her will haunt Cindy forever. She occasionally receives a phone call from his two daughters, and she still sends the girls birthday and holiday gifts. She told me that her biggest regret was that she couldn't have gotten visitation rights with them, too.

Be Careful When
Someone Asks for Money

Debbie came to me for financial advice and it didn't take long before I learned more about her than about her finances. A hard-working single mom living in a townhouse in a blue-collar neighborhood, Debbie was not much different from other women I met who shared the distinction of having married a bum.

He walked out on her when she was pregnant with their daughter, and followed up his bad behavior by refusing to support either of them—even his child. For the past five years, he was adroit at ignoring every court order Debbie initiated and, to add insult to injury, he didn't even bother to send cards or gifts on his daughter's birthdays. (Debbie tried to make up for her ex-husband's disgraceful behavior by signing his name to birthday cards sent each year to their daughter.)

Despite having had such a bad experience the first time around, Debbie remained open to finding a new relationship. She met Sam at a business networking event at a downtown law firm.

He was attracted to her from the get-go. How could he not have been? She was bright, attractive, worked as a junior loan officer at a prestigious Chicago bank, and was on a fast track to become a bank officer.

From the first night they met, Debbie found herself confiding in Sam about her struggles as a single mom and he listened attentively as she talked about creative juggling between her daughter's school schedules and work hours. He liked the fact that she had a strong support network; helpful girlfriends and a mom willing to babysit when necessary.

The two of them laughed about Grandma's propensity for indulging her only grandchild in junk food and computer games rather than Debbie's strict instruction that homework comes first! The fact that Sam seemed so open to listening to even mundane details of her life charmed Debbie.

No shrinking violet, Sam was a fast-talking salesman who smiled, laughed, and talked simultaneously. He told great stories and was charismatic, drawing people to him and making them laugh with his offbeat humor. Because Sam was a mortgage broker who owned his own small business, the two of them had lots in common.

Hours passed in a haze of delight as Debbie and Sam talked for hours, the party swirling around them. He talked her into leaving early and coming to his place. She hadn't had sex in years and, bolstered by several glasses of wine, wound up in bed. Despite his invitation to stay all night, she had to get home to her daughter.

Debbie and Sam dated every night for two or three weeks. Sam was exciting and fun to be with. Debbie could let her hair down and she adored the physical relationship that made her feel sexy and desirable again. Sam made her feel special. In his eyes, she was more than a working mom and she flourished thanks to Sam's attention.

Like all new love affairs, Debbie slowly learned more about Sam as the two grew closer. She learned about his two children from a previous marriage and admitted to me that she had begun to daydream about a future with Sam in which she would become a step-mom to his kids and they might even have a child of their own. After such a lousy marriage, Debbie still believed—somewhat naively, in my opinion—that a loving husband and financial security would make her life complete.

Floating around in the proverbial cloud, Debbie was almost impervious to Sam's faults. She saw him as a charming character who brought a lightheartedness to their relationship that balanced her responsible side, which is why, at first, it didn't register when Sam asked to use Debbie's credit card to obtain a loan and then also asked if she would guarantee his new car lease. He had explained that he was getting a new mortgage on real estate and did not want to damage his credit with the acquisition of new debt.

I'm pretty sure that Debbie noticed the look in my eyes when she shared this tidbit with me. I was struck by Sam's audacity. How could he make either of the two requests?

Thankfully, while Debbie remained in the afterglow of her love affair and their delicious sex life, her left brain hemisphere kicked in and she called me. I let her rave about her good fortune—about how lucky she was to have met Sam, who not only wanted to marry her but who had fallen in love with her daughter and wanted more kids with her.

"So, Larry—what do you think about my letting Sam use my credit card and co-signing his car lease?" she asked me.

I had to think hard and fast because I didn't disclose the fact that, in our small community, I knew exactly who Sam was and I also knew about his disgraceful track record. He had borrowed money from another woman who believed that she, too, was the love of his life and the eventual stepmother of his two daughters. I also knew Sam's ex-wife and had heard through the grapevine that not only was Sam always behind on his child support, he rarely saw his kids. Not the loving family man he portrayed to Debbie.

There's nothing in law school nor in my financial education that prepares someone in my profession for breaking news like this to a client, but I felt that I had to metaphorically rip off the Band-Aid fast. I told Debbie that Sam was a scoundrel. After comforting her as much as I could, I recommended running in the other direction and never looking back. She cried. She didn't want to believe me. But I kept talking to her and encouraged her to look at my motives: I was her friend as well as her attorney—why ever would I want to make her suffer? As she began to accept the reality I had interjected into her blissful life, she began to blame herself for being stupid. "Why do I find all of the shitty men on the planet?"

"Because you're a good person and you're too trusting," I said. "I can advise you on your finances and your legal issues, but sadly, I can't advise you about what to do about this idiot."

By the time I left her that evening, she knew what she had to do.

A few weeks later, Debbie called to tell me that while Sam kept calling her repeatedly, she knew what she had to do—for herself, her child, and her financial state. Neither Debbie nor I were shocked to learn, from the aforementioned grapevine, that it took him just weeks to glom onto another woman who was mesmerized by his funny stories and extreme attentiveness.

"You're going to find the right man," I assured her.

"I've put you on speed dial—just in case I do meet someone else who's too good to be true!" she added.

You Can't be Too Money-Savvy

Prior to her marriage to Steve, Joan worked as a certified financial analyst for a Wall Street firm. I knew her personally and professionally. Professionally she was able to dissect economic puzzles to predict future economic conditions. She had finely tooled macro- and micro economic instincts; her doctorate from the University of Chicago was so technical that I cannot tell you about it because I do not understand it.

Joan's good fortune extended to her personal life: She would tell anyone that she had married the love of her life; Steve and she were building a life that friends and colleagues held up as idyllic. Joan was so enamored with Steve that his friends joked she was like a robot forever saying, "Steve is my best friend and a good, caring husband." Then she would blush.

Because I'm something of a skeptic (due to the work I do and the wronged people I have met while practicing my craft), I used to roll my eyes whenever Joan went off on a Steve jag—until the day she came to me more distraught than I had ever seen her. When she told me that she had just found out that she had been financially duped by her husband, for years, I admit to being floored.

Joan retained me to be her forensic accountant; I girded my loins literally and figuratively. Having had so much experience working for women with Joan's credentials—yet who also turned a blind eye to partners and spouses in whom they implicitly trusted. I prepared myself for the worst as I picked up the boxes containing three years' of bank statements, brokerage statements, retirement statements, and credit card statements Joan had brought in for my review.

The room was so silent, the pages I turned sounded unusually loud. Finally, I looked up. "Why is it you never opened and examined the brokerage or bank statements to review the monthly balances and transactions?"

I knew what was coming, but I waited for her response anyway. "I trusted him."

"What about your joint income tax returns?"

"I—well, I just signed them without reviewing them." Joan's voice was a soulful whisper.

"What about the records and financials associated with your business?"

Joan and Steve had become skilled house flippers, buying up distressed properties and working with designers to refurbish and sell them at impressive profits. This business had not just made the two successful, but enabled her to keep a flexible schedule to take care of their kids.

Over five short years, Steve and Joan earned over two million dollars after taxes from flipping houses. Steve had an unrelated consulting business and earned another $300,000 per year. To save money, Steve and Joan lived in the houses while they were being refurbished.

Because their lives were so financially and logistically intertwined, this was going to be a long slog. Factor in the divorce now being negotiated between Steve and Joan and you can imagine the complexity of doing this audit.

Joan and I agreed that I would be retained to sleuth out the missing money from joint and personal investment accounts that the two of them shared while they were married.

My analytic process began by tracing cash that went into and out of bank accounts. Since divorce proceedings kicked in, Steve claimed that his business had fallen off, and his income was now less than $150,000 per year. I noticed that Steve had not disclosed his annual scheduled bonus and asked about it. Steve's attorney, after dodging the question, confided that it was being delayed until after the divorce was finalized—when I threatened him with a rule to show cause.

Steve was sly. He was looking for creative ways to pay less maintenance and child support by hiding scheduled bonuses of $50,000 from Joan.

I next analyzed brokerage accounts and perused bank statements and banking transactions. What stuck out most? There were numerous electronic transfers, each of which totaled under $25,000. These transfers methodically drained their bank accounts; so there were rarely available funds to be had and since these money transfers occurred several years ago, the job of sleuthing them out was going to be tricky, but not impossible.

I traced the monies to bank accounts—but not just any bank accounts. These were opened at institutions that had merged or failed over time and since the recipient's name wasn't disclosed on the bank statements, the new banks did not have those deposit/disbursement records. Even a subpoena couldn't get to the heart of these complex transactions.

I knew what I must do. The only person who could answer my questions was Steve. Since I was pretty sure he wasn't up for having a drink with me or a congenial chat, I chose to depose him at a deposition with a court reporter to record his statements.

Good idea—expected result! Steve could not remember any of the information regarding those bank transfers. His best guess was that the payments went to freelance contractors working on the houses he and Joan were flipping. In the name of being tidy, Steve also destroyed all records relating to their real estate transactions, but he took no responsibility.

"My tax preparer gave me that advice," he said. Steve did a lousy job of hiding his smirk.

Since there was no hard proof that a court would allow as evidence—and since we could not find the monies, savings accounts, or safety deposit boxes, I had little recourse but to move in a direction that could yield some financial secrets: plastic.

After tracing credit card charges Steve had run up over time, a pattern emerged that pointed to a gambling problem. Steve also had an expensive prostitute problem. He was an equal opportunity squanderer, yet those gambling and prostitution receipts that I was able to ferret out amounted to less than ten thousand dollars. On one check he was stupid enough to write in the memo section "sexual favors."

Steve knew the tricks of hiding income. He knew he could cash checks payable to third parties at currency exchanges to fund his little hobbies, but in the end, there proved to be in excess of two million dollars that couldn't be accounted.

I'd seen this behavior before and had to break the news to Joan that he had been planning for just such a circumstance. "He could have kept on going had you not noticed something fishy," I told her, hoping this might make her feel a little better.

But, is there such a thing as better when you find out that the love of your life has not only been skimming large amounts of money for gambling and prostitutes, but hiding millions? Sadly, the divorce court could not give Joan any financial relief to compensate her for his long-term and creative money management skills. And since there was zero proof that Steve misused most of the missing funds, we were dead in the water. We were able to prove only a small portion of the total and the court would not accept circumstantial evidence as to where the other monies were spent.

Joan wept as she left the courtroom on that dreary day.

Steve, thinking himself the cleverest guy on the planet, could not hide his grin.

Today, Joan is working hard to re-invent herself, despite years of being out of the workforce. Just last week, she called me to share that Steve had purchased a new Lexus before his business lost a major client and suffered a serious financial setback. "Oh, by the way," she added with a laugh, "I saw the Lexus being towed from his lot."

Does Money Change People?

After years of economic struggles, in concert with financial shouting matches with his wife, Jody, Bill agreed that their marriage was beyond reconciliation. Every night they argued over the same things: money and Bill. Jody complained about their inability to enjoy and afford vacations like their friends, a lack of retirement savings, and she even nagged Bill about a job he turned down years ago—a job that would have resulted in intense pressure that he would have hated, but it could have meant financial security if it did not kill him first.

As you can imagine, after a typical day of bickering, Bill and Jody's sex life was nonexistent and his insecurities began to take over his life. As a result, Jody countered by calling him unattractive and a failure, even in front of their kids. If there was a way to belittle him, she would. This intolerable situation left Bill in such bad emotional shape, he looked years older than his age, and it didn't help that he used food as his crutch. His weight gain drove Jody's latest round of insults. She enjoyed questioning his manhood, to the point where Bill would walk away like a beaten dog.

Jody ran a small cash business from home. I was called in to review accounting paperwork she had put together because a divorce was looming. They both desired to work out the financial issues and were willing to disclose their financial matters. Jody had been treating her home business as a hobby rather than an enterprise with profit potential; therefore, there were no records or receipts, just two or three numbers that she wrote down on a sheet of paper. Bill ordered me to accept these numbers because he assumed the business was unprofitable.

As we sat down at their kitchen table, we were able to reach a financial settlement and to agree on the non-financial issues too. They agreed to file the divorce Pro Se (without an attorney). A clerk at the courthouse assisted them with completing the paperwork. By filing Pro Se they saved money and did not deplete their meager savings. It was also hoped that this arrangement would cause their children less stress.

Because they agreed on most issues, filing divorce papers was a breeze and everything was finalized in a relatively short time. Jody stayed in the house and Bill found a nearby apartment, taking the basement furniture to furnish his new place to further cut his expenses.

Sound idyllic? That's what I thought—until a few months later. Bill arrived to pick up his children for their Wednesday night visitation. It felt weird ringing the doorbell at the house in which he had lived for so many years. After several rings and knocks on the door, his son Johnny opened the door timidly.

"What took you so long?" Bill asked.

"I thought you were Mommy. I spilled cereal all over the floor and I know she's going to be mad," he said.

"Are you alone?"

"She went next door," he said.

"Let me help you clean up," Bill offered. "Does your mom still keep the vacuum upstairs?"

Johnny nodded.

The two walked upstairs and pulled out the Hoover upright from the closet, along with a broom and dustpan. When he turned on the vacuum to start picking up the cereal, there was zero suction. Bill unzipped the back of the vacuum to check the bag. Instead of dirt and dust, Bill was shocked to find that the bag was stuffed to the brim with cash.

In that instant, Bill surmised that Jody's business was likely more profitable than she had let on when the two divided up assets before the divorce. It appeared she hadn't reported cash sales as income to Bill or me. Thanks to Johnny's cereal spill, Bill suddenly realized that he had some leverage. He didn't let on that he knew anything. After sweeping up the cereal, he wrote a note about taking the kids and left the house.

Bill didn't want the kids to overhear his conversation; so he waited a day to call me—after he had returned the children to Jody. I recommended he hire a private detective; his findings were even more revealing. Jody, it appeared, was running quite the successful business; socking tens of thousands of dollars away in safety deposit boxes at various neighborhood banks.

Apparently while Bill was eating himself into obesity, Jody was planning for a solo future. Her plan to divorce Bill and become self-supporting was must have been hatched years earlier, based on how long some of those bank boxes had been rented in her name only.

While legal constraints limited what the detective could prove, it wasn't hard to surmise her plans based on the timeline we drew up to track her behavior.

And this is also when something unexpected happened: As Jody was busy moving on with her new life, she began to shed friends like unwanted clothing. One particularly bitter friend decided to contact Bill and spill her guts. Jody, it seems, had shared her desire to find a successful and good-looking husband so she could be happy and live the life Bill couldn't provide. She ranted about finding a guy other women would covet—a romantic soul mate with whom she could travel and enjoy a privileged lifestyle.

It was now Bill's turn to get the upper hand. He confronted Jody about the vacuum bag filled with cash, but she played it cool and attempted to reassure him that the cash he had found represented profits found after the divorce. Bill could tell by her expression that she was playing him again. He had given her a chance to come clean and she blew it.

For a brief time, Bill was despondent, wondering if she had ever loved him. As his mind wandered, he even questioned whether or not she had been faithful to him. As his friend, not his attorney and financial advisor, I had to do some serious counseling to get Bill back on track. We had evidence that Jody had never been honest about her earnings and at first; he wasn't willing to pursue her legally. But when I asked Bill what sort of example he was setting for his kids and for his own self-esteem, by rolling over yet again, I think it hit home.

On that day, Bill began to formulate a plan to see if we could prove that the financial affidavits that disclosed Jody's assets and income were, in fact, falsified. Bill brought a petition before the judge to re-open the case on the grounds that Jody had committed fraud.

Was Bill able to make good on that claim? Not really. But Bill seemed to change as he felt empowered. He was no longer a punching bag willing to take anything Jody was prepared to dish out. He lost some weight and started to look healthier and younger.

That alone gave Jody pause. Frightened that she would wind up in jail after losing all of her assets to lawyers while the fraud threat loomed, she capitulated and told her attorney that if Bill would drop his fraud claims, she would agree to lower his child support payments and end his maintenance obligation. This capitulation did more for Bill's ego than anything else.

Did I know the fraud allegations had no legs? Yes. But I enjoyed watching Jody lose her hold over Bill.

Both went on to re-marry. Last I heard, Bill was blissfully happy and Jody was busy discovering that the man she chose was less than advertised!

What Would You Do for Money?

Roger is a good-looking man. He is well-groomed, loves golf, drives a new red Jag, and enjoys his martinis. Roger plays golf at a private, exclusive country club where members are from the Donald Trump set. Because he has a great personality, Roger is enormously popular and has loads of friends. Too good to be true? Of course. He has one fatal flaw: the moment he spots a hot woman, he comes down with a serious bout of *Marriagus Forgetus*. That's my code for: he has no recall of Mary Ann, the wife who waits for him at home.

Mary Ann ignored rumors for some time, but eventually, she became fed up. She filed for divorce, informing Roger by text messaging that a summons and a petition for divorce was going to be served.

It's hard to believe that Roger hadn't prepared for this eventuality, but he seemed incredulous when he forwarded the text to me so I could ready Mary Ann's pithy message: "You will be served with divorce papers. You shouldn't have a problem finding another bed to sleep in; your personal stuff is boxed up in the garage."

Moments later, Roger forwarded her addendum: "You can see your children if you can pry yourself away from the whores."

As Roger's attorney, I had to be his advocate; thus I was aware of his most recent office flirtation with young and adorable Missy. She knew Roger was the poster boy for lechery (who didn't?) but he was terribly charming and the most successful broker in the office. While she didn't date older or married men, she eventually gave in because he paid so much attention to her.

As their friendship grew, Missy began to have money issues. Her father died, she became responsible for taking care of her mother, and the student loans that dog today's college graduates perpetually hung over her head. In passing, she mentioned her frustration to Roger.

Her timing was nothing short of serendipitous. Roger had been trying to figure out ways to cut his tether to Mary Ann and it dawned on him that Missy's vast knowledge and technical insurance expertise, particularly when it came to her income and estate tax planning skills, could be his solution. Roger needed an ally; someone he could trust and work with. He thought Missy would be the perfect partner in crime.

Was Roger being beneficent? Hardly. He needed to reduce his income and was hatching a clever plan that would result in serious cuts to Mary Ann's child support and marital mainte-nance payments. Of course, hiding income while working for a huge, prestigious insurance firm was no walk in the park. But he had a plan.

Roger approached Missy. At first, he asked if she still wanted to earn more money than she was currently taking home. He hinted that he was willing to mentor her and set up a business relationship in which she would assist him. He invited her to talk specifics over dinner at Reggie's, an upscale eatery, thinking it would impress her.

The two had cocktails and Roger let Missy talk about her ambitions. He knew that she had no wealthy connections but she certainly had the personality and brains to become success-ful; so he shared enough of his personal story to see how she responded.

"I'm in the midst of a divorce; so I'm making many personal changes in my life to achieve new goals," he said. "You seem like a kindred spirit. I'm wondering whether I can help you achieve your goals, too."

Missy perked up as she looked across the table and realized that he was talking about becoming her mentor. At least, that's how she read his intentions. By the time the server brought the check, Roger had Missy in the palm of his hand. He also wound up in the palm of her bed. Mission accomplished.

Within a day or so, Roger took Missy aside and rolled out his grand plan. "I'm going to provide you with eighty percent of my new business leads," he began. "I'll help you prepare your pre-sentations to win over my financially secure referrals, send you to meet them, and seal the deals."

"What's the catch?"

"I'm putting all of my cards on the table because we need to be able to trust each other if we go forward," Roger explained. "I need to reduce my income while I'm in the midst of this divorce mess, but once it's history, I'll be expecting you to return to me half of your post-tax commissions."

Missy's expression didn't change as she mulled the details of his offer. "Is there more?"

"Yes. If I need money over the course of the divorce action, I will ask you to provide it under the table. No checks or ways to trace these transactions. Once the divorce is final, you and I become full business partners and we prosper together."

Roger looked into her big brown eyes as she asked if that was everything he wanted to say.

"No. I want this partnership to exist on multiple levels."

Translation: he also wanted Missy to be his lover.

At first, she hesitated. Sensing her pull back, Roger added, "If the arrangement doesn't work for you, we call it quits and you transfer the files and clients back to me. But if that happens after the divorce action is over, you keep the clients and everything you've made, less my share."

Missy may have been young but she knew a tempting deal when she heard one. Say yes, she thought, and you get money, mentoring, and a successful future. Chances are, she would never get an opportunity like this again.

But sleeping with Roger felt like a deal breaker; so she tried to put that aspect of their proposed arrangement into perspective. "Roger, you are so good-looking, you can have any woman you want. Why would you want to sleep with me exclusively?"

He smiled enigmatically, as if to say, "I'm offering you the deal of a lifetime. Ball's in your court."

"If I agreed to the proposal, will you agree not have sex with other women? I don't want to catch any diseases."

In that instant, Roger knew that Missy had taken the bait and all he needed to do at that point was to reel in his catch. By agreeing to remain faithful, no easy task, could Missy overcome her reservations?

In the end, Missy pointedly said that she was willing to sell her soul as long as Roger was a man of his word. Their pact was sealed.

True to his word, Roger proved to be an outstanding teacher and mentor. He taught Missy how to close large life insurance and group health insurance deals, analyzed and instructed her on improving and refining her sales presentations, and extended his advice to cover her wardrobe and social skills when meeting with clients.

To Missy's surprise, he wasn't bad in bed, either. That doesn't mean that Missy simply eased into this sexual liaison without self-recrimination. At first, it was difficult. She felt like a skank, but as she settled into this aspect of their relationship, she had to admit that the sex was amazing. Her body craved his touch regularly.

Meanwhile, the money that was flowing into her bank accounts helped mediate the remaining moral issues she hung onto, and in the end, Missy developed a fondness and respect for Roger—in both the boardroom and the bedroom.

Time passed. The divorce dragged on. Roger's and Missy's business relationship thrived and it wasn't long before monthly commissions of $20,000 or more made their way into her bank accounts. On the other end of the continuum, Missy's understanding of the ways to satisfy the needs of high-roller clients grew exponentially.

In fact, Missy liked to joke that she had become a better version of Roger! She now possessed poise and sophistication that continued to elevate her status and, unlike Roger, who wasn't as eager to succeed, Missy did the little things that endeared her to her clients. She took pride meeting with them. She routinely explained the fine points of policies. Eventually, many of Roger's clients preferred dealing with Missy.

At the end of two years, Roger told Missy that his divorce was finalized. Roger hoped that they would be able to continue the arrangement, and he even proposed moving in together, suggesting they might get married down the road. She asked for time to respond.

A few days later, the couple went for drinks. His expectations were high. How can she resist me, now that she's learned to look at life through my eyes? he thought.

"I have learned much from you, and I will always be grateful to you for helping me surpass even my wildest dreams. I have a financially successful practice and I have even learned how it feels to be sexually satisfied."

Roger's expectations went up another notch as Missy continued to flatter him. "I have been totally loyal to you as a friend, student, and lover."

She placed her hand on his and lovingly stroked it. "As for living with you and marrying you, one of the biggest lessons you taught me over the past couple years is that this relationship—personal and professional—won't last forever. I don't want to hurt you, but we both know this is true. I have all of the skills I need to build my future and I want that future to be with someone I can trust and love forever."

After putting cash on the table to cover the tab, Missy slid her purse over her shoulder and stood up. He was too shocked to move or say anything when she added, "I can't have a business and life partner with someone I honestly can't trust."

In that moment, Roger realized that Missy knew him all too well. He had fallen in love with someone who could never love him in return, based on the nefarious arrangement that was at the foundation of their partnership.

Now, he knew how his ex-wife must have felt.

When Roger called me to share his tale of woe, I patiently listened, because that's what lawyers on the clock do. I didn't mean to be disloyal when, after I hung up the phone, I said aloud, "Good for you, Missy!"

Court Orders Can be Good

When John and Joan came into my life, the two of them were relatively successful. He earned about $100,000 as an assistant controller and Joan earned around $100,000 per year as a self-employed consultant. Further, the couple had marital assets consisting of: two cars, $250,000 in savings, and a home with some equity.

I was representing John at the beginning of their divorce negotiations and, at first, I couldn't believe how amiable they were. They agreed to equally split the $250,000. Things were even easier as we moved forward. My suggestion that Joan and John each pay their own attorney fees, without seeking court approval, proved another victory.

One thing I did recommend, however, was getting a court order to spell out the terms under which the money would be split. Both John and Joan shook off my suggestion. They wanted a clean split and didn't feel it was necessary to do more than just split those assets down the middle.

Was I thrilled? Hardly. This was beginning to remind me of cases I had handled where one party insisted they were so in love and sympatico, a pre-nup wasn't needed. My response? A more professional version of "Oy." But, my job was to follow my client's wishes; so we moved ahead.

This case, I thought, was going to be a walk in the park. But my park walk ended the day John called in a panic.

The divorce was about to be signed, sealed, and delivered and John just learned that Joan had spent her half of the savings on "business and living expenses" and had nothing left of the original $250,000 the two of them had split. Say what? She had blown $125,000 in twelve months?

I could understand why John was in panic mode, but I wasn't prepared for what I heard next. Joan's attorney was claiming that John's $125,000 was still considered marital property. Joan now demanded that John's half be split between the two.

I couldn't see his face as he shouted into the phone, but I assumed it matched his pithy utterance of: "You got to be fucking kidding!"

I had to calm him down as I shifted gears from being only his divorce attorney to being his divorce attorney and forensic CPA.

John retained me to trace, discover, and verify what Joan had done with her original share of the previously distributed monies. John was sure Joan was hiding monies in an undisclosed bank account or safety deposit box, but it was all speculation. At the moment, my job was to keep John calm enough to do my job.

Joan's attorney had, at this point, moved into what I like to call "threat mode." He demanded that the $125,000 be immediately split 50/50 or "we're headed for a lengthy trial." John, it seemed, was given forty-eight hours to decide. I bought us some additional time, hoping I would turn up a money trail. In fact, I came up empty-handed.

I always want to get the best deal possible for my clients, but in this case, we were up against a wall. With no court order to fall back on, I sat John down and spelled it out: either hand over the $65,000 and move on or be prepared to spend around $50,000 for trial expenses and at least another $10,000 for the forensic accounting fees required to fight this.

"If Joan is telling the truth and the money is gone, you're going to wind up forking over $60,000 in professional fees and still owe her $65,000 if you lose. Do you want to cut your losses and keep some of your money or risk winding up without a cent?" I asked.

To save John the embarrassment, I did not deliver an "I told you so" soliloquy by pointing out that a court order might have nipped this whole thing in the bud. He was suffering enough.

In the end, John gave Joan the money and settled the case; though I did have to talk him down when he asked me if he could write "Blood Money" on the check!

I'm delighted to report that John moved on with his life. And chances are, if someone mentions "court order" in the future, he is going to say yes. Another expensive lesson learned.

Do Not Marry
the Prince of Persia

Susan was born and raised in a small town in Southern Illinois' Bible belt, where she was fortunate to have strong family ties despite having very little money. She was the first in her family to get a university degree; a first step to becoming the nurse she had dreamed of becoming ever since she was a kid.

Smart and pretty, Susan continued to make her childhood dream come true by landing a great job as an operating room nurse at a busy hospital. She met well-respected surgeon Raja where many medical professionals do: over the body of a patient being treated for a trauma.

Raja was twenty years older than Susan and his worldview was quite sophisticated compared to hers, since he was born abroad and educated in the United Kingdom. Even their appearances were dramatically distinct. She could have posed for farm calendars—the fresh, blonde, and blue-eyed face of innocent beauty.

Raja looked like he could attend a movie casting call for *The Prince of Persia* and win the role hands down.

Recently divorced and the father of a fifteen-year-old daughter, Raja immediately became enraptured by Susan's sweet demeanor and warmth. He dramatically swept her off her feet by taking her out for lavish dinners and showering her with gifts of jewelry.

He introduced Susan to his family, some of whom had just emigrated from India—and even introduced her to his faith by exposing her to the Hindi culture and belief systems. It was just a matter of time before she converted to his faith and married Raja at a suburban temple.

The honeymoon? India, of course. There were still more relatives to meet and he insisted on taking her to the Taj Mahal, perhaps the most romantic palace on the planet. They were hardly back from their honeymoon when Raja began urging Susan to start a family. He had a daughter but wanted sons to carry on the family name.

In keeping with this idyllic portrait the two of them were painting, Susan produced not one but two healthy sons in rapid succession and acquiesced to his compelling request to quit nursing so she could stay home and raise the boys. He gave Susan $2,000 per month for house expenses and two credit cards.

Unbeknownst to Susan—until she checked the income page of the income tax form she usually signed without reading—she learned that Raja had earned a whopping $900,000 that year. Seeing those numbers was a jarring experience. In that moment, she became acutely aware that she knew nothing about their finances. She had a checking account into which her monthly stipend was deposited and that was it.

Can a woman come to the realization that she's being squeezed into a state of isolation if the process is done so slowly it's almost undetectable? Not always. But with nothing to complain about, it was easy for Susan to just keep living what her friends called an "enviable life."

By the time they celebrated their 18th wedding anniversary, Raja began making subtle comments about Susan's age. Although he was approaching sixty-three, he insinuated that, at age forty-three, Susan was getting older and he was bothered by it. Having molded herself and her life around his wishes and desires, Susan was both hurt and frightened.

Their relationship grew even tenser when Raja began maintaining strange hours and acting differently. Susan assumed that his behavior was her fault and she tried to be more attentive, thinking that might revitalize their relationship. But no matter how she tried—no matter how much sex and passion she brought to their bed--he acted as if he was doing her a favor and placating him when the two made love.

Like all simmering pots, water cannot be stopped from turning into a full boil if left on the burner long enough, and that's exactly what was about to happen with Susan and Raja. One weekday morning out of the blue, he called Susan and asked her to hire a babysitter for that evening and invited her to meet him at one of their favorite restaurants at 7 p.m. Susan was overjoyed. A nice dinner; just the two of them. She couldn't recall how long it had been since she had felt this hopeful.

Dressing in Raja's favorite outfit, Susan met her husband at the appointed time. He had already ordered drinks and she loved the fact that he always remembered the wine she loved. Surely things were turning around.

Their wine glasses half-emptied, Raja leaned in close to Susan and said, "Susan, I want a divorce. I've met somebody and fallen in love."

At first, Susan laughed, assuming he was joking. But the look on his face said it all. She stared at him, stunned and unmoving. It was too much to take in. Around her, diners chatted and laughed in this surreal environment in which she was asking her brain to come to grips with his request—but her thoughts were too jumbled.

"Look, Susan, once we're divorced, you're going to have plenty of money. I'll pay you $4,000 monthly for maintenance and $2,000 monthly for child support for three years. I'm also prepared to write you a check for $15,000 right now—to help you get resettled," Raja explained quietly.

"How long have you been planning this?" Susan asked, as tears began to fall and she felt the world crumbling around her.

"Is this necessary?" Raja responded, in his usual calm, rational voice. "Tell me what you want."

She wanted to forget that this conversation had ever taken place. It was evident she was so shocked, she was in no shape to discuss settlement terms.

"Susan, I need to move on."

To add insult to injury, Raja began telling Susan about his twenty-six-year-old girlfriend; also a Midwest-bred nurse working at a nearby hospital.

"Enough," she finally managed to say, before getting up from the table and leaving the restaurant. When she returned home, I was her first phone call after a friend recommended me because I was both a practicing divorce attorney and a forensic CPA. She needed both and was wise enough to admit it.

When we met in person, Susan filled me in on all of the details—particularly Raja's offer and his veiled threat that she either acquiesce or he would move his assets and money to India, leaving her not only penniless but without the resources to fight an international battle.

"If I don't act quickly, he's got me over a barrel," she pleaded. "Can you help me?"

Things didn't look good. Not only was Raja threatening to take his assets to his homeland but he was also threatening to move himself and the girlfriend there, too. It seems he had already updated and renewed his licenses back in India and was prepared to take any of the many offers he had been receiving of late.

Given his time in the U.S., Raja had a unique set of skills and experience. A man with his talent and training was always in demand, said his lawyer when the two of us spoke. "Your client has a profession. All she needs to do is upgrade and update her credentials and she can work as a nurse and make a good living," he said. "My client is happy to pay for college educations for their kids. It's a great offer," he added.

Susan was scared. For the past eighteen years, she existed only to please her husband and take care of their children. For the first time, she admitted he was physically abusive whenever she challenged him. Her behavior and demeanor were typical of what I'd seen in battered women. Raja had played on every one of her insecurities. She would be penniless. Alone. Washed up at the age of forty-three. She remotely considered suicide.

I wished I could offer her more hope, but Raja had Susan over the proverbial barrel. He could easily take his income and assets abroad and obtain his divorce in India even; well before the Illinois court system could begin divorce proceedings that would wind up in a bureaucratic wringer. Bottom line: unless he was served, the Illinois courts would not have jurisdiction over him.

Susan didn't need me to tell her that she was in deep; so it became my job to make sensible recommendations after assuring her that things weren't hopeless because we had options that included asking the court for preventative measures that would stop him from liquidating his 401(k) and work-related pension plan. I explained that we could get copies of income tax returns from the IRS and we could subpoena paychecks from the hospital to learn where he maintained bank accounts, but I warned Susan that this would require patience because it could take weeks.

Susan was worried about paying me almost as much as she wanted to have options; so I reassured her and suggested three scenarios:

"Option one is accept his deal, knowing that, based on his income, an Illinois court would award you close to $350,000 annually plus fifty percent of the marital assets.

"Option two is to accept his offer and then return to court claiming that you accepted the offer under duress and ask the court to provide assistance and protection.

"Your third option is to immediately file for divorce, have him served, and then file an emergency petition to have both his pension and the house secured while we keep searching for his assets."

Just hearing that she had options seemed to put Susan into a more relaxed state. When I added that whichever option she chose, we'd also make sure that Raja paid for my services, I could see that the weight of the world had just dropped from her shoulders. Her face lit up with a huge smile.

Since this particular matter is still being litigated, I have to leave you hanging, but I had to include this story for a reason: sometimes my job is more than just undertaking divorce details, sleuthing out hidden assets, and coming up with creative ways to serve my client. Sometimes, figuring out how to reassure a client that she's not alone and has someone fighting on her behalf, as I did for Susan, can be the biggest service I render.

Money is Everything

Martha and Robert managed to stay married for thirty years—long enough to send their kids to college and get them started in life, thanks to his wealthy parents who were in a position to help out.

But, like so many couples that have been together for decades, Robert had long ago fallen out of love with Martha—even before she became seriously ill and was required to take numerous medications that dulled her mind. Robert's depression grew as he faced long-term medical costs associated with Martha's deteriorating health and, since her mental healthcare was not covered by insurance, he vacillated between feeling depressed and desperate.

Robert turned to his wealthy parents, who hired attorneys skilled at drafting agreements to create gifts and to transfer assets from Martha under the guise of tax planning. Martha signed the documents while being heavily medicated. With the stroke of a pen, she gifted her share of the marital residence and Robert's business to his siblings in a trust for the benefit of Robert and

Martha's children. In this way, the family would be protected when Robert filed for divorce.

Blissfully assuming she would be taken care of by her husband, initially Martha was placid and trusting—but as time passed, she developed an irrational fear of dying at the hands of Robert's family.

Was it intuition, fantasy, or simply the result of side effects from taking powerful medications? Her fears grew palpable. She envisioned Robert's mother taking a long knife to stab Martha in the back and imagined that her life was in mortal danger because someone was tampering with the drugs she was taking.

She so feared for her life, she locked her bedroom doors at night, and occasionally called the police. After a while, local law enforcement authorities ceased to respond immediately because she had earned the reputation of being crackpot.

Things reached crisis stage when Martha grew so paranoid, she couldn't stay at home. Robert gave her some cash and helped her move into an apartment, adding a cruel condition to his offer to support her in her new place: he insisted that their children choose sides. "If you side with your mother, you're going to be cut out of your inheritance and your jobs at the family business won't be waiting for you," he told them after delivering this news to Martha. The children chose to align themselves with their father.

Martha was now alone, without family or friends. She found the abandonment by her children to be emotionally catastrophic and the medicines furthered her downward spiral. It took a suicide attempt for Martha to realize she really wanted to live, despite her circumstances.

That is when I entered the picture.

When Martha first called, I knew it was taking every ounce of courage she could muster just to pick up the phone. I sensed her desperation. Even before we met in person, I urged her to apply for disability and Medicaid until we could get her back on her feet.

Frankly, when I heard about how Martha had been treated

by her husband, in-laws, and children, I felt disgusted. I couldn't recall a client who needed help as much as Martha. Without ever having met any of them, I developed an irrational dislike of them all.

I informed Martha that we would not only pull out all stops to reverse the marital estate rights that had been pulled out from under her, but I would initiate divorce proceedings on her behalf and my fees would come out of the monies collected from the family.

She seemed skeptical, but I told her I was confident we would win; and if we didn't, I'd chalk my fees up to the proceeds of a pro bono case. Later Martha told me that she got her deepest sleep the night we prepared to do battle against Robert's high-profile family that had deep community roots with mayors and judges on speed dial.

Talk about a challenging job, even for a forensic accountant! The family business was a cash-only enterprise; thus most the family members' incomes never made it to their tax returns. They were in deep—Robert lived in a multi-million dollar house owned by his parents.

The family's lifestyle wasn't too shabby, either. Both Robert and the children traveled extensively and enjoyed luxuries that ran from high-end cars to designer clothing. And they entertained lavishly.

I am at my best when I'm out for blood, and I was mightily inspired by the callous treatment these wealthy people had exhibited toward Martha. When Martha and I arrived for our first court date, their counsel table was so full, I was reminded of the O.J. Simpson dream team.

No matter. We were ready.

Robert was called on to present his side of the story; his performance was worthy of an Academy Award. He told the court he was living on loans his parents had given him because the business was in such a bad state it was perpetually on the brink of bankruptcy.

Attorneys had prepared Robert for the role of a lifetime. He falsely admitted to being a lousy businessman and appealed to the judge to evaluate his position with as much heart as head. "I'm keeping this business alive only so my children have futures—I have confidence that they will work hard to turn things around and see the day that the business turns a profit."

Robert's attorneys had brought banker's boxes full of financial statements that attested to the decades of loans bestowed on Robert by his parents. There were few records available to verify the cash the business had taken in and its use.

As for Martha, by the time this reached the courts, she had been through something of a metamorphosis. Her Medicaid benefit had kicked in and a new doctor put her on medications with fewer side effects. She had gotten a part-time job for the first time in over thirty years and it was evident from the way she told her story that this woman had come up against untold odds, yet managed to keep her dignity and carve out a life for herself.

The judge ruled that there was no proof the family business was a profitable enterprise, though he complimented the convoluted money management system the family had so creatively used over the years. No evidence was presented to indicate that Robert had a source of income except for the family loans. The judge's decree ordered Robert to pay a minimal amount of maintenance, a one-time settlement of cash for Martha's future, and my fees.

Martha knew she would be forever destitute and had to decide if she wanted to continue a life in pain. Robert and the kids packed their bags to vacation in Switzerland.

Section V

Court Rulings:
How to Throw Predictions
out the Window

Sometimes
There is a Tax on Candy

Gary and Grace were high school sweet-
hearts in the Illinois farm belt—where corn, not sugar, was the
cash crop. More ambitious than their friends, they decided to
move north where success, they were convinced, awaited them in
the Chicago area.

Neither were accountants (nor had they received a formal
business or financial education), but what they lacked in financial
skills, they made up for in creativity. They launched a small candy
store strategically placed near an elementary school and a high
school.

So successful were Grace and Gary, it took less time than they
first projected to turn their simple idea into a flourishing, profitable enterprise. Kids loved candy and had pocket money. (I'll
spare you the puns; insert them on your own.)

The couple's simple idea morphed into a small chain of similar
candy shops. Emboldened by their good fortune, and with cash
flowing in like an endless faucet dispensing pure cane sugar, Gary

figured he was born under a lucky star. When it came time to file income taxes, he dutifully reported the business's net income, his six-figure salary, and living expenses. Any remaining funds were invested back into the business.

When the Illinois Department of Revenue came knocking on their door and announced that they were there to perform a sales-tax audit that covered the past three years, Gary said he had nothing to hide…unless you count his lack of tax expertise, which is why he had no clue that each of the couple's three stores were situated in areas that had different sales-tax rates.

When the audit was completed, the news wasn't easy to swallow: Gary and the business owed the state $150,000 in sales tax. Ever vigilant, the federal government learned about the state audit and initiated an audit of their own; this time it involved the corporation's employee and payroll taxes.

Things got dicey. It seems that part-time employees were being treated as independent contractors; a serious no-no in the world of federal business audits that revealed this violation of tax laws. Gary and the company were asked to pay back payroll taxes in addition to monies owed to the State of Illinois.

You have no need of more details. Suffice to say that the amount of tax, penalties, and interest from the two tax audits forced Grace and Gary into a rather exotic form of bankruptcy known as a "confession of judgment." What's so great about a Confession 11 bankruptcy? It's fast. So fast, if circumstances are right, you can be in and out within three months.

Settling into a somewhat blissful state, Gary and Grace promised to abide by conditions set while under the protection of the Confession 11 Bankruptcy. Needing money to pay vendors, Gary and Grace religiously agreed to set aside cash from store sales when they learned of the tax problems. Old habits die hard. During the bankruptcy and thereafter, the couple added to their cash savings. The pair failed to report their cash savings to the Bankruptcy Court and, after the bankruptcy, they continued to cook the books and accumulate unrecorded sales.

They stashed a big box in their clothes closet—$90,000 during their first post-audit year—but they grew careless as creditors demanded to be paid before they delivered goods.

And then, there was that box filled with $90k in small bills lurking on the closet floor.

In the game of Candyland, players race through Candy Cane Forest and Gum Drop Mountain to get to the Candy Castle first, but in the Gary-and-Grace version, there were no winners. The trauma of the business going belly up left Grace so emotionally devastated, she left Illinois for a warmer climate and took the kids, blaming Gary for everything. She stashed the $90,000 in the trunk of her car.

Once she established residency, she filed for divorce, leaving Gary behind to clean up the mess. He was forced to declare personal bankruptcy. A trustee sold the couple's residence and forced Gary to move into his pickup truck. Gary showered every morning at the $25-per-month health club in the neighborhood.

It got worse. To make a living, in his forties, Gary sought work as a handyman. He had learned carpentry and handyman skills from his father as a teen and this seemed a logical money-making avenue since he had no formal education and his job prospects were, to be kind, limited.

But here's where I separate Gary from so many of my clients. He took responsibility and set about rebuilding his life by advertising his handyman services on grocery store bulletin boards, Craig's List, and in free shopper newspapers. His truck remained his office and residence as he saved money for an apartment.

If Gary wanted to be vindictive, he could have named Grace as the mastermind behind that big box of cash that Grace had also relocated to her new home in the south, but why compound the tragedy? After all, he was a co-conspirator and didn't want to go to jail any more than he wanted to send Grace to jail.

Wryly, Gary said that his truck wasn't big enough for the kids too.

Sadly, Grace wasn't as generous. In her divorce petition, she claimed that Gary still had the ability to earn a six-figure income, but claimed he chose not to do so. As a result, the court ordered

Gary to pay more in child support and maintenance than he was earning from his construction jobs. Using copies of Gary's old W-2 forms as proof of past earnings, she went after him with a vengeance.

Gary no longer had to worry about living out of his truck, saving for an apartment, and scrounging for jobs. His inability to pay the court-ordered child support and maintenance resulted in an arrest warrant, courtesy of the State of Illinois. The sheriff arrested Gary and locked him up in jail.

After thirty days, Gary was able to get a hearing and convinced the court to reduce his financial obligations; so off he went to a life that had him working sixty hours per week in an effort to stay current and out of jail. He does feel a bit queasy every time he passes a candy store.

The Grass Might Not be Greener

Like so many other businesses, Frank's
was affected by the recession. Not only did he lose customers, his
accounts receivable list was so long, it had passed the point of
being collectible.

Frank held on and did his best to ride out the recession without firing any employees. Unfortunately, he didn't apply the
same reasoning to his lifestyle; mostly because he was afraid to
tell his wife, Judith, that they were broke. His infrequent idea to
get a job was almost immediately dismissed because, at his age,
his prospects were bleak.

Some people are happy to face the music, make drastic
changes, fess up to their better halves, and get on with their
lives—but Frank didn't happen to be one of them. He started
to dip into payroll tax funds earmarked for employee withhold-
ing. By the time the IRS caught up with Frank, he owed at least
$100,000 in back taxes.

I'm not sure how Judith learned that the IRS had come

calling, forcing Frank to reduce his salary, but I'm glad I wasn't in the room when she got the news. Judith didn't take the news that they would have to reduce expenses and sell their home in good spirits.

What does a woman who has never been told no do when confronted with this situation? In an effort to save herself, Judith came to me and wanted me to represent her in a divorce action.

Talk about a conflict of interest. I'd been their financial advisor for years and now I was being asked to get into the middle of their divorce which, to state it mildly, was going to be an exercise in mud wrestling.

"I married Frank for richer, not poorer," she callously said when the three of us met to see if we couldn't sort things out reasonably. Her comment startled Frank so much, his jaw dropped and he was left speechless.

As you can imagine, there was no mediating this contentious situation, and Judith took my efforts to set some sort of a conciliatory tone as my "being on Frank's side." I no longer had a conflict of interest. Judith hired another attorney and we began the dance of judge selection.

It's no secret that some judges tend to rule on behalf of wives more favorably, just as there are judges who more often than not uphold the husband's side of the story. The dice was thrown and we were assigned someone in the first category. It was going to be an uphill battle.

Judith told her attorney that Frank had stashed money away for a rainy day. It wasn't true, but Frank was responsible for trying to disprove that these rainy-day savings didn't exist. Meanwhile, the court awarded temporary maintenance to Judith based on Frank's previous year's earnings, thereby negating the financial restraints dictated by the IRS.

It had become my job to explain the new financial realties with the IRS, but the judge didn't care. Judith's attorney pointed to the company's retained earnings and told the court that Frank could use those monies to pay the taxes. Such retained earnings are historical profits and the judge, an idiot in my opinion, didn't fully understand that the company was insolvent.

We were up against a wall. Frank's obligations to the IRS and court-ordered maintenance were greater than his income; so we had to return to court and again plead for a partial reduction of the maintenance. It was Frank's only avenue as the IRS wasn't willing to wait. Because he was boxed in, Frank defaulted on Judith's payments, the court denied the motion, and threatened Frank with contempt of court and possible jail time.

We were given 90 days to figure a way out of the crisis that amounted to Frank either losing the business or being jailed.

More drama lurked on the home front, where Frank and Judith both still resided, because a buyer for the house had yet to be found. I warned Frank that nothing good was to be gained by living under the same roof, but he said he had no other options.

One night, the couple got into a screaming match over their financial situation. They both reached a profound state of frustration. A concerned neighbor called the police.

But even a police presence didn't turn off the faucet of threats, curses, and mean-spirited accusations that somehow culminated in Frank threatening the officers. Not only were neighbors privy to the soundtrack, but they also had an opportunity to watch a handcuffed Frank being shoved into a police car.

Judith signed a complaint, charging him with threatening her and she was thereby granted an emergency motion for court protection that required Frank to stay a specific distance from both the residence and Judith. Unable to move back into the house, Frank began sleeping on his office floor and showering at his health club. He was now officially one step up from a street person.

By some miracle and/or divine intervention, Frank and his business survived the recession. Judith was granted her divorce and we managed to settle the maintenance situation by seeking redress with a different judge who based her payment on his actual income, not the money he made during their days of wine and roses.

Today, Judith lives in a small studio apartment. Frank has gotten back on his feet, lives comfortably on his reduced income, and finds life to be as peaceful as he's ever known it without Judith. While he says he wouldn't wish his IRS experience—nor his trip to jail on domestic abuse charges—on anyone, he says that he learned a great lesson: when compared to a demanding ex-wife, the IRS is a walk in the park.

You Can Fool
the World, But Not Me

After many years in a terrible marriage, Jerry moved out of the couple's home and hired me. I listened to his story and agreed that years of abuse had taken a toll on him and it was in everyone's best interest to split up.

Soon-to-be-ex Janice had a mild case of arthritis that was controlled by medicine. In my opinion, Janice used her doctor more as a sounding board than a medical professional, because during every visit, she regaled him with tales of how Jerry beat her up and threatened to deny her the medical treatments she needed to control her arthritis. She begged the doctor to help her.

Janice tried her best to persuade the divorce court that she deserved a healthy financial settlement by bringing in her doctor as a witness. He tried to do the right thing in his heart by embellishing the severity of Janice's actual medical condition. Emboldened by his testimony, Janice began to milk her condition for all it was worth, pretending to be more and more debilitated every time she showed up in court.

I had to stop myself from laughing at a hearing to settle a minor matter in which she showed up at court wielding a cane and using the cane to make the agonizingly slow journey from the door of the courtroom to the bench. Call me jaded, but I swear, her limp grew more pronounced with each step. When she finally arrived, Janice's tears flowed with wild abandon. It was obvious that the judge was moved by her suffering.

Poor Jerry. I say this as both his attorney and the witness to Janice's award-worthy performances. The case dragged on so long, I began writing off a percentage of Jerry's bills as pro bono work. At the four-year mark (I've had cases that dragged on longer), we got a break. The judge was transferred to another court.

My mother said the same thing your mother did: Be careful what you wish for.

By this juncture, I was wishing for any judge with the ability to see through Janice's theatrics; and while I thought I had already seen the extent to which she was willing to carry on her charade, even I wasn't prepared for her next act.

New judge on the bench, the courtroom door swung open, and a great deal of noise filtered in that caused everyone to stop what they were doing and turn around. There was Janice, in a wheelchair, pulling a three-foot-tall oxygen tank on a dolly. The tank looked as though it had been borrowed from a movie set in which World War II was being re-enacted. On her face, Janice wore a plastic mask and an oxygen cannula hung from her nostrils beneath the mask. This time it was Jerry who had to resist the urge to laugh out loud. The only thing that kept that in check was fear that the new judge might find him callous to the point of developing a dislike for my client from day one.

Doing what could be called the world's best imitation of a stroke victim, Janice's head hung to the side as her wheelchair was placed in the center of the courtroom. I noted that even Janice's wardrobe was selected with care: she wore an old cotton housedress, her hair was unkempt, and not an iota of makeup had been applied to her face.

Jerry and I looked at each other with unspoken words: Nicely orchestrated, Janice.

Of course, her attorney was behind this charade and, as he began to explain to the judge his client's need for medical care 24/7, because she was barely able to function, I could see the knuckles of Jerry's hands grow white. I avoided looking at his face. I knew what I'd see: frustration, despair, and disgust. We had a new judge but an old ruling: Jerry was ordered to comply with motions for additional financial aid based only on her demeanor.

We happened to be outside waiting for a cab when both of us caught sight of Janice jumping from the wheelchair held by her attorney into her SUV and leaving the scene. She had no problem driving herself home. Despite our best efforts, this scenario played out with annoying regularity as her "condition" continued to deteriorate with each court appearance.

I knew that Jerry was broke, but desperate times call for desperate measures. I proposed hiring a licensed private detective for a last-ditch assault on the truth. To my surprise, Jerry not only agreed but said, "I'll borrow money to pay for your investigator—I don't have anything to lose at this point!"

Seeing the hope on his face, something I hadn't seen in years, I got my guy on the case and he was charged with a single directive: follow Janice and document her activities.

For days we heard nothing. Jerry told me that every time his cell phone rang, he nearly jumped out of his skin. I didn't want to alarm him, but the investigator's findings were on my mind, too! I had grown weary of watching Janice screw him over; and while I know it's not professional to admit this, I wanted her to go down for making my client so miserable and for so long.

At last, my phone rang, and I called Jerry to get over to my office as soon as he could. He jumped in his car and by the time he arrived, I had set up my computer in our conference room. All that was missing was the popcorn and soft drinks. We were about to watch the show.

Aided by his verbal description, the investigator took us through a week's timeline, accompanied by unmistakable photos of Janice in action. One day, she went to pick up their kids from camp and she helped them load luggage into the back of her SUV with the ease of an airport porter. There was no sign of oxygen, canes, or a wheelchair.

To greet her kids, she had dressed nicely in jeans, a shirt, her hair had been styled, and her makeup was perfect. As a matter of fact, the only video footage we saw in which Janice wore no makeup was when she went out for her daily run. Our PI caught her moving heavy lawn furniture, schlepping heavy bags of groceries, and exhibiting full range of motion as she went about her day.

We were going to sleep really well that night—all three of us. Between the 150 still photos and extensive video footage, we were officially prepared to go back to court—only this time, on our terms.

As usual, Janice presented a pathetic picture upon entering the courtroom for the latest round, but I did note a look of panic in her eyes when she took in the screen we had set up and the table that held the computer that would deliver our evidence.

But first, we gave her the gift of perjuring herself. As she moved haltingly to the witness box and continued to convey the latest chapter in her soap opera, it was hard for either of us to contain our glee when Janice's lawyer finished guiding her in her latest appeal to get more money this time for a full-time caregiver and a car service since she was no longer able to drive.

I didn't bother to cross examine her, putting my investigator on the stand instead. He explained his assignment and then smoothly transitioned into the monologue that accompanied the video now playing on the large screen.

I could see the judge's jaw begin to work as he watched Janice in action. The horror on her face spoke volumes.

Accusations of "violation of privacy" flew from the mouth of Janice's attorney, but it was a last hurrah. I hate using the cliché here, but it's too appropriate to leave unsaid—pictures really are worth a thousand words.

I don't remember the last time I saw Jerry smile, but on that day, he was beaming. Janice was admonished by the court for her deceitful behavior, as was her attorney. With the Sword of Damocles hanging over both of their heads, the judge not only issued an order that stripped Janice of most of the relief he and the former judge had granted, but he promised not to forget those images if she ever showed up in his court again.

I took my investigator and Jerry out for celebratory drinks. It was the least I could do for them both!

Even Blissful Relationships Can End in Risky Business

April and Bill were married for eight years. Together, they launched a breeding and training farm for racing horses that took all of the cash they could muster, including their savings. As I often say, youthful exuberance of the hopelessly optimistic is a great thing to experience. Since the demand for breeders and trainers happened to be high, just about everyone who knew the couple had high hopes that just one winning horse could generate the kind of revenue that would answer their financial prayers.

What usually happens to people with so much riding on an enterprise and no cushion to fall back on? In my opinion, it's almost impossible to sustain a relationship when the sole focus of a couple becomes a business. As a result, while the business stayed afloat over the years, April felt neglected. She had hoped for children and a loving relationship. Instead, she wound up with a husband whose obsession with work knew no bounds.

"I love Bill," April said when she turned to me for legal advice. "But there's no passion in our marriage, and I want more." Bill, so involved with the business, had no clue this was coming. He was hurt and shocked. The couple agreed on a quick property settlement to get April off to a new start and Bill could heal and continue to devote all of his time to the horses.

A year passed. Far as I knew, April was re-inventing herself and enjoying her life as a single woman. But Bill was in trouble because he had spent another year without a winning horse. Circumstances made it necessary for Bill to find a replacement jockey; and he found one in the form of a young man who worked at the stables who felt confident that his talents were being wasted training rather than competitively riding horses. Bill didn't have any other options, so he auditioned him.

Does good fortune strike only after a person has been put through a ringer? That's my theory. To Bill's shock and amazement, the replacement jockey won not one but two races on two of Bill's horses. Watching him come out of the gate, Bill noticed that this young man's style was much more aggressive than his nephew's.

"You're amazing," Bill said as he pumped Jose's hand while the two stood in the second winner's circle. "I don't have a lot of money but I would certainly be interested in hiring you to work for me."

Despite Jose's broken English, he had no trouble understanding Bill's offer of employment. "I will take minimum wage plus a share of each purse," he said, and the deal was struck.

Jose rode Bill's horses to numerous victories and showings, but Bill was caught completely off-guard when, a year later, his horse 312 was invited to run in the Kentucky Derby. Suspecting that someone was playing a trick on him, he dialed the Derby offices and learned that the invitation was indeed authentic.

Things got rosier: 312 won an enviable lottery position. As the third horse from the rail, he would be adorned with emerald green colors, the number 7, and even a four-leaf clover. As you can imagine, all of these signs converged to convince Bill that, at long last, his luck was about to change.

On race day, and with the start out of the gate just hours away, Bill and Jose discussed tactics. Feeling grateful to have come this far, Bill told Jose that he was more than just a jockey in his eyes—that he also considered him a friend.

"No matter what happens today, I'm never going to forget what you've done for me," he told Jose, shaking his hand and patting his back.

While Jose prepared for the race, Bill headed for the coffee shop, stopping dead in his tracks when he saw April coming toward him. Not only did she look fabulous, but she was very pregnant and looked content. Bill had heard that April married another breeder; as it turned out, her husband's horse would be running against 312! His first thought was to walk the other way, but before he could change direction, April called to him.

Bill smiled and walked over, feeling somewhat tongue-tied and awkward, but April immediately bridged the gap by coming up to him, giving him a big kiss on the cheek, and a warm hug.

"Look at us," she said with a big grin. "I hear your wishes have come true and your horses have been so successful!"

In that instant, he wanted to say he was very happy with his life, but in fact, he realized he missed her terribly. The two exchanged small talk and as he began to relax, he even told her that he was happy for her.

It was obvious, even to the untrained eye, that the two of them still had feelings for each other, but it was just as obvious that this wouldn't change the reality of their situations. With a baby due in weeks, April joked, "I just hope this season ends before this child decides it's time to greet the world."

Bill laughed and responded, "Well, you never know when a foal will decide to come out—they don't ask permission!" They both laughed.

"I hope you don't mind me staying in touch with your mom and your sister," she added. In fact, neither family member had mentioned this to him—perhaps they didn't want to depress him or cause him any sadness. "I'm so glad that they've remained healthy and happy."

Checking her watch, April reacted with mock horror that the two of them had been chatting for so long. "I've got to go, but before I do, I just want you to know that I wish you all of the luck in the world today." He could tell by the tone of her voice that she really meant it.

As she turned to leave, April looked back. "I have never stopped praying for your happiness," she said. "And I hope you know that I have always loved you. That's not going to change," she added, walking away.

At exactly that moment, Jose ran from the stable, grabbing Bill's arm to tell him that he had to report to Derby headquarters immediately. His head spinning, he walked in the direction of the office and tried to shake off the emotion that overwhelmed him.

Years later, he still recalls walking into the Derby office to take care of some paperwork with tears in his eyes. A clerk looked up at Bill. "Don't cry," she said. "You and your horse can always come back next year."

"But we haven't run yet," he said.

"My, aren't you an emotional and sentimental man. Your wife is lucky to be married to you."

If only she knew.

Section VI

IS It Stealing IF
the Victim iS Your Spouse?

Never
Underestimate a Clever Conniver

Tom, a forensic CPA and my client, struck up a conversation with the woman sitting beside him at the waiting area in a Walgreen's pharmacy when the pharmacist called her over to tell her that her prescription was ready. When asked for payment, rather than taking out her wallet, she said, "My ex-husband set up a Walgreen's account for me so I can charge the children's medications to his credit card on file here."

The clerk looked up the account and found it, but before he rang it up, the woman stopped him. "May I use the Walgreen's charge to pay for prepaid VISA and other credit cards that Walgreens sells?"

"Our accounts aren't limited to medications," he said, pointing out a woman who was putting her meds plus food and toys on her tab.

Light bulbs went off in Tom's head as he watched this exchange. His marriage had been on the rocks for years, and I was handling his divorce.

When we talked later, he asked me whether or not the Walgreen's charges appearing on one credit card statement every month in the amount of around $700 could be from his wife putting aside money in the form of prepaid cards.

"Clever," I recall saying, making a personal note to check statements from pharmacies more carefully in the future while undertaking a forensic audit of an opponent's records. And, for the moment, it sounded like Tom needed me to take off my lawyer hat and put on my CPA hat.

As I roamed through the files Tom's wife had submitted, I found a trail of unusually large charges at Walgreen's, over many years, that had slipped through as being the result of one of their children's illnesses When asked about the charges, she always stated, "What do you think I did with the money? Look at the VISA bill. It says Walgreens and a dollar amount."

"I never thought to question my wife when she kept telling me that our insurance company didn't cover so many of our son's medical costs—I mean, wouldn't you believe it?" lamented Tom.

I nodded my head sympathetically but offered no response because years of watching clients' spouses come up with creative ways to skim money undetected had left me a bit—well, jaded. I asked Tom to contact Walgreen's and request three months' worth of detailed purchase register tapes detailing each purchase.

Tom asked the clerk to produce the last three months' register tape details; he was told that the clerk could only extract the details of purchases made within the last thirty days. To his surprise, his wife had charged $750 that consisted of $15 in medications and $735 in prepaid VISA credit cards.

Given the fact that we are both accountants, the revelation turned both of our brains into casino slot machines as we began to do the simple math. "She could have racked up $20,000 in the last three years," Tom said, beating me to the conclusion.

In that moment, I saw on Tom's face what I like to call the "gloves off" expression. "I feel like an idiot," he said to me. "I should have known those bills were too high, but I never asked."

"Don't feel like an idiot," I responded as I patted him on the back. "If I were to gather together every client I've worked with who was taken for this kind of ride, I might have the money to rent the United Center," I said, referring to the cavernous facility that served as home to the Chicago Bulls basketball team.

As I began to investigate more closely every bill Tom's wife submitted to the court, I must admit I grudgingly developed a certain admiration for this woman's chutzpah. She had even found a way to get reimbursements for vet bills in the form of reimbursement checks while Tom paid the premiums.

I'd love to put a cap on this story for you, but it continues to drag on through the courts. Tom's wife has plenty of prepaid credit cards stowed away; so as long as she has a source of cash, the case will continue. Tom now pays all medical and drug bills related to the kids directly. I keep assuring him the cards will eventually run out and that he did the right thing by paying, without question, the expenses he believed were for his children's medical needs.

Friends Will Help
You Cheat on Your Wife

Beth's divorce attorney asked Carl to explain the cash withdrawals from his bank accounts and on his credit card statements. Carl explained that he always needed cash to pay for small business purchases, like office supplies.

Mysteriously, those cash withdrawals went from $100 per week before the couple filed for divorce to between $400 and $500. Carl's explanation? He was using extra cash to promote his business since he needed to offset the costs of the divorce.

Sounded logical to me; so even though I was Carl's attorney, I didn't think this increased outlay would be controversial. Additionally, in light of his newfound efforts to grow the business exponentially, he also dined and entertained potential and existing clients using cash rather than credit cards.

Did I think this was a great idea? Hardly. But as Carl's counsel, my job was to advise not dictate, so just to stay in practice, I occasionally reminded him that using his credit card for business dealings whenever possible made good legal sense.

And, like my kids, he continued to ignore me.

Two years before the divorce was filed, Carl and his buddies planned and schemed. Because Carl and Beth had been married so long—and had known each other and their close circle of friends for as long as they could remember—there came a time during the divorce dance that there was a shift in friendships. Carl got custody of the divorced guys. Beth forged alliances with their ex-wives.

In addition to getting together over bottles of wine and whining, Carl came to rely on his close friends for their advice on how to minimize his income in order to pay less maintenance and child support. "I don't know," said Carl to his pal Jack, when Jack offered creative advice on hiding income borne of innovative transactions the group had begun to use.

"Beth knows about our group's little enterprises. We were still married when the group helped you screw Anne out of a bigger share of support than she would have received if those records were not bogus. She'll know that you guys are going to want to help me target her next."

"Obviously this calls for some new ways to stash cash," Jack laughed. And so the plot thickened as the contingent of divorced men began to come up with a web of loans, mortgage transactions, and other financial finagling that would allow Carl to continue to hide assets. They even signed and recorded mortgages related to real estate owned by Carl and Beth so it appeared as though the title to their home was improperly completed and required corrections. Beth never looked twice at the document while signing it. Because at the time she thought they were happily married and she trusted Carl.

Beth's attorneys took the deposition of the "friends" and subpoenaed copies of checks and proofs that payments were made from the friends to Carl and Beth. One friend claimed that his basement flooded last year and the paperwork was destroyed. Then he couldn't recall which bank account on which the funds were drawn.

Carl couldn't locate bank statements reflecting transactions either. I reminded him that all of these shenanigans could land his too-clever butt in jail for false testimony. Like most schemes, things began to unravel without warning.

During a friend's deposition, he told the court that he planned to loan Carl money and would expedite the mortgage process to accomplish just that. Further into the deposition, he accidentally admitted to applying for a credit card for Carl's benefit.

I always tell clients that single-word answers are preferable when on the stand. I'm not sure Carl's friend had received the same education because later in his testimony, his elaboration included the phrase: "Carl regularly uses this card." There were a few objections, but the torture continued. "Carl gives me cash and then I pay the credit card with one of my checks," the friend offered.

Like a dutiful representative, I kept the objections coming as I slowly began to imagine how my client would look dressed in standard prison garb—but of course, every prison is different and perhaps his ass could still be saved. The death knell came when the attorney asked for the credit card statements, only to be told, "I throw them away every month."

"Well, how about giving me the name of the credit card company."

"Objection!" came my knee-jerk response.

Before the judge could rule, Carl's friend responded, "Oh, I canceled that card two months ago." Things went downhill from there and included unsavory details that ranged from Carl entertaining paramours using his friend's credit cards to reimbursing them in cash.

It was obviously too tempting for Beth's attorney to take a pass on this sudden detour in testimony because he switched the topic from credit card scams to women. I had run out of Perry Mason moments by this point—until the name Nancy was introduced.

Nancy, it seems, was Carol's coworker. Single and in her late thirties, she actually fell for Carl and saw him as her soul mate. The two launched a torrid affair in hotel rooms, where the two indulged their shared fantasies. When they traveled together, they booked adjoining rooms to maintain some propriety, but things escalated even more at that point.

When, at last, Carl decided that he had had enough of Beth and was ready to move onto Nancy, he asked his paramour if she would help him in his effort to divorce, so the two of them could be together at last. From the grin on her face, Carl knew he had successfully enlisted a new scam buddy, only this one came with benefits.

Nancy happily followed his lead by taking commissions from projects he spearheaded and putting them into her own account, giving him back his share after taxes. Nancy was dewy-eyed and in love; she felt privileged to help Carl out so they could be together.

Carl continued to sow seeds of exaggeration by telling Nancy all about Beth's spending sickness; tales that began as minor truths that were embellished into a fabric of finely woven lies. Given so many reasons to help Carl, Nancy was a willing participant in this charade as Carl continued to manipulate money like a seasoned Vegas card dealer, all the while hiding plenty of money and reducing his income on paper to almost laughable amounts.

I wasn't anywhere near Nancy when she received a subpoena for documents and was called in for a deposition. As Carl's attorney, I obviously couldn't represent her; so Carl decided to prep her himself rather than hiring an attorney to help her.

"Play dumb," he instructed Nancy. "If they ask about our relationship, tell them we went out for drinks occasionally." Unfortunately for Carl, the reason he was attracted to Nancy in the first place was that she was sweet, naïve, and incapable of lying.

Excuse the cliché, but my best assessment of her performance on the stand was that Nancy folded like a deck of cards. As a matter of fact, she helped pour the cement over Carl's grave, metaphorically speaking. By disclosing their asset "relocation" system, every last detail of the scheme came to light.

At this point, Carl would need the next coming of Jesus to

extricate himself from this mess. I urged him to try and settle using my most persuasive arguments and fearing that, once again, Carl would insist on being seen as the smartest man in the room—he finally took my advice.

What happened to Nancy? Carl dumped her forthwith, since she was no longer useful to him. Beth took Carl to the cleaners; and, of course, he did what he did best: blamed me for the trouble that awaited him as fraud charges were being brought.

By the time Nancy's testimony had been applied to the fraud case, things were looking grim. The karma train, it seemed, had pulled into Carl's station at a nice rate of speed.

Playboys Love Themselves

When people ask me about my scariest case, the face of Charles, the dude whose lifelong desire was to marry for money, flashes across my mind.

Charles received the same sort of upbringing as did the UK's Prince Charles, minus the crown. He never met a country club he couldn't crash and maturing was last on a long list of things he hoped to avoid. He even admitted that his sole ambition was to be a playboy and hang out with gorgeous women; the younger, the better.

Charles identified with actor Walter Matthau, who starred in the movie *A New Leaf*. If you missed the film, Walter's character decides to marry for money and murder his spouse to inherit her wealth, but he fell in love with her and wound up saving her life instead.

But Charles was nothing like the character in the film. He hadn't an iota of sympathy or compassion for anyone but himself, and now, he was starting to run out of money thanks to his lavish spending habits; so he knew it was time to launch his action plan to lure a wealthy woman.

No rocket scientist, Charles's brilliant plan included dressing his age, pretending to be childless, and acting respectably to give everyone the impression that he had grown up. Charles spread the word to friends and family that he was ready for a serious relationship, and he began showing up at summer parties in wealthier areas of the country like the Hamptons and Cape Cod.

At each appearance, he reconnoitered the "field" with the diligence of General Patton, honing in on women with significant family wealth. Charles still had good looks and personality—so much so, the women flocked his way and his contemporaries were envious; yet they were happy to act as his surrogates at events he wasn't able to attend.

In advance of most parties, Charles obtained copies of the guest lists and made discreet inquiries, sometimes running financial histories of the women who appeared to be his best marriage bets. Thanks to social media, he learned plenty about each one, and when all was said and done, Samantha became his number one target.

She was an interesting woman on many counts. She had played competitive sports at an all-girl high school and attended a small private college. She sailed her own boat and traveled the world. Charles felt an immediate attraction thanks to her considerable wealth—and she wasn't bad looking.

As luck would have it, Charles's friend Michael grew up with Samantha, so introductions were made at the next social event. While she had some trouble holding her own when they conversed, Charles picked up the slack. He was happy to control the conversation, ask questions, and open her up.

"Would you like to join me for tennis at the club on Saturday morning?"

Samantha was taken aback. He was speaking her language. Surprising even herself, she agreed.

While playing tennis, Samantha was on familiar turf. She had no trouble talking while she played and seemed to enjoy herself because there was no pressure. Charles likes to say he let her win that day, but in fact, she out-played him and he was happy to hand her the victory.

Athletic endeavors became the key that unlocked Samantha. They set a second date to play lacrosse with friends at a local field. Their third date took place on her sailboat. Charles brought a few bottles of wine with him in a wine cooler and the beverages did plenty to relax her.

Charles romanced her to the point that she was sexually open to him and he quickly knew that his long-range plan was working. She even told him, on a particularly romantic night as they sat on the balcony of her high-rise, that she believed she had finally found her soul mate.

He was in.

The relationship proceeded in high gear. After more weeks of dating, he was invited to the family estate for Sunday night dinner. It was an opportunity for her parents to formally meet and talk with Charles, who dialed up his charm to "high" throughout the visit.

Six months later, they announced their engagement. They decided to have the wedding ceremony at an old Spanish church on New Year's Eve on a Caribbean island. All was love and rose—until forty-eight hours before the ceremony when Samantha's father insisted that Charles sign a prenuptial agreement requiring a decade of wedded bliss before Charles could receive financial benefits from their marriage, should he seek a divorce.

The prenuptial agreement stated that all of Samantha's assets, plus assets she was due to inherit or be gifted, were to become the property of a credit shelter trust for Samantha and her heirs. If Samantha died prior to having children, her siblings inherited.

It got more complicated, as these sorts of documents tend to do: If Charles remained married to Samantha for more than five years and if she died of natural causes, Charles would get $150,000 for each year of marriage.

This document was shoved in front of Charles's face after everyone showed up on the Caribbean island. I wasn't around to vet it—nor was anyone else—so he signed the document without having a clue about the terms it contained.

"I'm signing this without reading it because I love Samantha," Charles said to her father as he thrust a pen in his direction. He thought he had played that rather nicely, in fact. Who could imagine that he wasn't marrying her for all the right reasons? So, he wouldn't get his hands on any money as quickly as he might want, but he liked to think of himself as a patient man.

As fate would have it, Samantha proved to be the perfect wife for Charles. Her trust fund enabled the couple to travel the world—spending time among the finest resorts, hotels, and restaurants. She even surprised him with her ability to handle a racing car in the French Alps and he would never be able to match her skiing skills, but eventually Samantha grew tired of all the travel and wanted a conventional life with a home and kids.

Conversely, Charles made no secret of the fact that this was the life he wanted. Bits and pieces of his true nature began to be revealed, as was his immaturity. But, he obviously wanted her content, so when she suggested investing some of their wedding gift money into a real estate project he named "Sam's Dream," she thought he was about to transition into the life she craved.

Sam's Dream would be co-owned by a friend named Stephen whose goals in life approximated Charles's. Stephen would be the partner who played along without asking too many questions as the life insurance sales scheme morphed from idea to practice. In addition to sucking naïve buyers into their trap, Charles put into place a buy/sell agreement that authorized the purchase of life insurance policies.

That's how Stephen came to hold policies on Samantha's life. If Samantha died, Stephen would buy Samantha's shares for the policy amount with proceeds paid directly to Charles rather than her estate. The face amount of each policy? A cool seven figures. Truth is, Charles had to admit to an emotional attachment to his wife, and he wondered, if push came to shove, whether he could choose between her and an insurance payout.

He wouldn't have to wait long to make the decision. On a

rather warm but moonless summer evening, about twenty-five couples gathered on the deck of a yacht that belonged to one member of this circle of friends. It was actually the last gathering of its kind before everyone returned from their vacations to jobs and families awaiting them in the city.

As parties tend to do, this one went from lively to raucous between the time when they set sail in the afternoon to past sunset. The floating bacchanal had taken on a life of its own.

From her deck chair, Samantha sighed as she looked over the rowdy crowd. She was bored and listless, and it didn't help that Charles and Stephen had spent the entire voyage in conversation at the other end of the boat. Was it her imagination or did the two look conspiratorial, she wondered. They kept glancing over at her in between Charles's solicitous trips to her chair, fresh cocktail in hand.

With zero desire to emulate all of the idiots behaving badly, she preferred to play observer. And since she thought she might be pregnant, she stealthily dumped every cocktail overboard as soon as Charles headed back to Stephen. With each return visit, she smelled pot and booze. It dawned on her that she had shoved her Kindle into her purse; so she dug it out and jumped into the book she was reading.

From his vantage point, Charles grew annoyed. "I don't get it. She's had enough drinks to inebriate an elephant and there she sits, reading as if she hadn't had one," he said.

Stephen was fairly tanked and had nothing to offer; so he nodded solemnly and continued to watch guests as they laughed, danced, ran up and down the deck, and generally acted like the spoiled people they were.

Alcohol-infused chatter was the order of the day; so when a woman Samantha knew came to sit down at the foot of her deck chair, she turned away from the book.

"What are you doing over here all by yourself, Sam?" she demanded to know.

"I'm afraid I'm not in much of a party mindset," she answered.

"Well, you need to reel in that husband of yours. There's a

rumor going around the boat that Charles has been bragging to some of the trophy wives on this excursion that he'll be coming into some big money very soon. Of course, the wife is always the last to know!"

Samantha looked over at the two men as they continued to sequester themselves. For the first time, she felt suspicious and unsettled. Things weren't feeling kosher. For reasons she still doesn't understand, Samantha used Charles's password to check out his financial files on her smart phone. What she found would have been enough to sober her up—had she been drinking. She realized they planned for her to swim with the fishes.

Asking the captain to take her ashore in the speedboat that had piloted guests to and from shore all day long, she slipped away. Charles figured Sam had gone below deck to use the loo, until he caught a glimpse of her, in the little boat, speeding away.

Her first call upon reaching shore was to her father. As for Charles, he was stuck on the yacht until it returned, giving Samantha enough time to pack and head for the airport, where she took the first available flight back to the states. His calls to her mobile phone went unanswered.

When Charles returned to shore, he raced to the hotel, but her bags were gone and there was no note in sight. The front desk clerk informed Charles that she had taken a cab to the airport. Now, it was Charles who raced to gather his things, but by the time he got to the airport, she was gone.

Upon arriving at their residence later in the day, Charles found his belongings packed into boxes that awaited him at the curb. She had been so efficient, even the locks were changed on the doors. Awaiting him when the door opened to his furious knocks was his father-in-law's attorney.

"Let's be clear," he said. "You are no longer welcome at Samantha's home and I've taken the liberty of printing out a copy of your pre-nup. I'll need an address so I can send you a copy of our proposed marriage dissolution agreement once it's done. Please review it with your attorney and have him contact me. Now, leave the property. You are trespassing."

For two weeks Charles attempted to contact Samantha, but was told she chose not to speak with him.

He did, however, reach me. All I could tell him was: "Charles, I reviewed your pre-nuptial agreement after the fact and warned you that you should have run it by me before you signed it. Right now, all I can do is check out whatever divorce papers you receive to see how I can help." I didn't mean to be cruel but there was truly nothing else I could do for him at this point in time.

Charles, meanwhile, was off on a flight of fancy, convinced he could con his way back into Samantha's heart, but she was so insulated by staff that he couldn't as much as get her on the phone. He became so persistent, people began to hang up on him; yet he remained clueless, thinking that he could convince her he was repentant and she would take him back.

At last, he managed to get an appointment with her attorney, but as usual, he opted not to bring counsel (that's me). Awaiting him was Samantha's father and Mr. Barnes, Esq. settled in high-backed leather chairs. He took a seat and started to speak, but his father-in-law beat him to the punch.

"Charles," he said, "the marriage is over. The question is whether you will have some walking away money. Do you have money to waste on legal fees, my boy? Personally, I find attorneys a legal necessity but if we go in front of a judge today, you'll get nothing because you weren't coerced into signing. Here is my proposal: You never see Samantha again. If, on the off chance, she's pregnant, you relinquish all parental rights forever."

As usual, Charles said nothing; so his father-in-law continued. "My attorneys have drafted a dissolution of marriage agreement. Read it carefully or bring it to an attorney. Your choice. How much money do you want?"

Charles thought a minute and asked for $150,000. I know what you're thinking: why didn't he phone me or stall until I could vet the document?

The amount was agreed upon, Charles did what Charles usually did: he signed on the dotted line without having read a word of the agreement. He willingly signed a document saying that he agreed to the settlement amount and a secretary swooped in to witness and notarize it. His father-in-law asked Charles for a bank transmittal number so he could wire the $150,000 directly into his bank account.

Charles hadn't even thought to ask about that "relinquishing all parental rights" business because he was too busy thinking of himself. No birth announcement arrived at his mailing address six months later, either. I like to think that the kid just dodged a bullet. Charles? He was already in hot pursuit of a new mark by that point.

Sex is Important?

Mary was a naïve nineteen-year-old when she married Robert, a divorced thirty-five-year-old, after meeting him in a shared law firm's common kitchen and conference room. He was looking for a relationship that included the exciting sex he missed after marrying his first wife. What made Mary so desirable? She possessed both innocence and external beauty and it was his greatest desire to be her teacher when it came to sex.

Mary was swept off her feet by the sophisticated guy dressed in designer suits who seemed to be well-educated and personable—and it didn't hurt that he also appeared to be wealthy. Their flirtation went on for weeks before he said, "I'd ask you out if there wasn't such a big age difference."

"I'd be interested," Mary laughed, inviting him to ask her out.

Robert took her to dinner at a trendy restaurant after work one Friday, but once there, Mary felt out of place, wondering if her outfit was appropriate. She had no clue that she was the most beautiful woman in the room. A bottle of wine relaxed them both and as dinner ended, knowing that she lived with her parents, he asked, "What time are you expected home?"

Her response: "The night is young."

"Good girl. Where shall we go tonight?"

She suggested taking a cab to Chicago's Navy Pier or walking along Michigan Avenue in the Oak Street Beach area. While strolling the shore arm-in-arm, she spontaneously turned to him and gave him a passionate kiss. And so, the romance began.

It took no time at all for sex to up the ante on their dating life. Mary proved to be all he dreamed about because she desired nonstop sex and there were times he wondered if he could keep up with her appetite! His passion morphed into something of an obsession. She and her lithe body dominated his thoughts day and night.

Robert was a guy who liked to show his affection by spoiling a woman. He took Mary shopping for clothes and introduced her to the concept of a personal shopper trained to help customers select the right garments. When Robert picked up the tab during each of these shopping expeditions, she felt like Cinderella. He upped the ante by buying her jewelry to match her outfits.

As time passed, Mary began to question her motivation. Was she attracted to Robert or his affluent lifestyle? She admitted to herself that she had had much better lovers in the past and she wondered if his attraction lay more in the financial security he seemed to offer than the love she usually craved.

That answer came when he proposed marriage. She accepted and the two settled into their respective roles.

Eighteen years passed. During that time, Mary remained beautiful and young, but Robert's looks were fading and his sexual performance required the assistance of medical science. She was able to compensate for these changes by becoming heavily involved in charitable work, sitting on boards, and making a name for herself on Chicago's philanthropic scene.

Mary also found that her creative talent for decorating was also cause for lots of admiration; so with Robert's encouragement and a collapsing real estate market, she quickly discovered that she had a talent for home flipping, buying distressed properties and renovating them for resale. That's how she met John.

As a contractor, John was everything a house flipper could want. He was a whiz at all aspects of home renovation, was mindful of getting quality products at reasonable prices, and he actually showed up on site when he said he would.

As a man, John was everything Mary wanted at this stage of her life! Young. Handsome. Employed. A Good Sense of Humor. She quickly realized that she was wildly attracted to him and even began fantasizing about him on the infrequent occasions she and Robert had sex.

John felt the same way about Mary, but the flirtation dance they were enjoying was just too delicious to move to the next step; and so, they continued in this state of sexual limbo. Realizing that she had a lot to lose if she violated the pre-nuptial agreement I had urged Robert to sign when he told me he was going to marry Mary, proved a powerful force every time the urge to rip off John's shorts (when he worked, he usually wore nothing else) became too strong.

If she was unfaithful to him or wanted to divorce Robert, her financial benefits would dissipate and there would be no more charitable board seats, renovated homes, or John time. However, if Robert was proven to be unfaithful, she could wind up with a hefty income for life. Had he been unfaithful? Mary suspected that he had begun to roam in recent years, but Robert was clever and she hadn't found any telltale signs.

That's when I factored into the equation. Mary was referred to me by a friend. Since I'm a forensic accountant and an attorney, she thought that my credentials worked for her. She asked if she could retain me as a start to the plan she had in mind: get out from under the onus of her pre-nup by laying some infidelity groundwork.

With a healthy retainer fee in my corporate account, I turned loose one of my favorite investigators and he proved to be a gold-mine of information. Robert's latest fling, according to initial reports, was Julie, a sharp, attractive twenty-eight-year-old who had become enamored of Robert when the two met at a business function. She expressed interest in learning more about Chicago real estate from Robert, who qualified as one of the city's finest entrepreneurs when it came to residential and commercial properties.

Julie was young and beautiful and she had a propensity for wearing short, seductive skirts. Her biggest asset? She had no desire for a lifetime commitment. She didn't believe in them. Her future, she wasn't shy to admit, would be invested in obtaining a mentor who would insure her financial success.

My PI conducted a variety of background checks on Julie and once he began to become familiar with the couple's meet-up patterns (yes, even careful cheaters develop patterns), he was ready to swing into action. The envelope filled with surveillance photos were all Mary needed to get out of the marriage. What straw broke the camel's back? The snapshot showing the two canoodling at the restaurant to which Robert had first taken Mary.

Now that we had plenty of evidence, divorce proceedings could begin, but we needed to put some more ducks in a row before we filed; so I counseled her on what she could reasonably ask for based on their financial records. Wanting to inflict maximum damage, Mary directed me to have him served with their order of dissolution at his office—once I talked her out of having the process server follow Julie and Robert and serve him while they were together!

We managed to get Mary a nice financial settlement that ran in the millions; so she could move on with her life. Did she then proceed to get into a torrid affair with John, so the two of them could do more than renovate houses? You'll have to use your imagination, because as her counsel and financial advisor, my lips are sealed.

Section VII

EFFective WayS to Drive PeopLe Crazy

You Must be Kidding

While many married couples seem to specialize in make-up sex following disagreements and estrangements, Sam and Debbie went to the opposite end of the continuum as a result of their souring relationship: they had no sex for years. With each other, that is.

Both carried on affairs and found satisfaction in the arms of others, but it was a strangely choreographed dance of denial as they had these discreet liaisons with others, yet never acknowledged that they knew of the other's affairs.

Since I had represented Sam and Debbie, both confided in me about their current state of affairs. Both felt guilty because the true love they once felt for each other had withered and they had given up trying to rekindle it. I played marriage counselor and talked them into admitting that they couldn't go on like this, helping them to admit that divorce was the only answer.

From my perspective, that was the easy part. I offered to represent them both in the action and at first they welcomed the thought that this could be handled quickly and without rancor. But it took no time at all for both to start pointing fingers and uttering statements about wanting the other to "pay" for the failure of the marriage.

I'd seen it before. I'll see it again. The bridge of agreement the three of us had built collapsed before my eyes as I watched the two of them commit to destroying each other during the divorce process, regardless of the emotional or financial toll.

A divorce action like Sam's and Debbie's often reminds me of a football game. The coach requires forty-eight minutes of punishment and effort until the game plays out and ends. In divorce terms, Sam and Debbie were poised to pull every dirty trick in the book—and some that had yet to be written—until the judge granted the divorce.

How much time did it take before their children were roped into this nasty dance? Next to none. Both kids attended a Jewish day school and Sam and Debbie began to use them as battle weapons. School officials could barely keep track of the ever-changing custody arrangements as the temporary maintenance skirmishes raged on. I was having trouble keeping track of the custody and visitation calendar changes, so just about everyone remained confused.

What broke the loggerheads? Debbie. Her decision to move the kids from their Jewish day school to a Catholic school proved the ultimate slap as she took aim at Sam in the most creative way she could conjure up. Her radical plan was aimed at driving Sam crazy and forcing him into a quick settlement with better terms. She was so bitter that she didn't care that Sam's parents were Holocaust survivors.

As fate would have it, when things crashed and burned, there was no way to represent both of these angry people and I wound up taking Debbie's side. Was it a mistake? You could say so. I knew it the moment she looked at me with a smug smile and described how she transferred the kids to a parochial school leaving Sam and his parents devastated.

This was a declaration of war. Sam immediately went to court to try and stop Debbie from putting the kids into the Catholic school. The judge listened to their arguments. Debbie explained that the Jewish day school cost over $20,000 per child per year while the Catholic school ran only about $6,000 for each, thus we were able to show that the tuition was far less expensive.

Debbie further told the judge that while there were some excellent public schools in the area, they were hard to get into, what with long waiting lists due to smaller class size. She explained to the judge that the lottery system to get into these institutions was daunting.

The judge could find no downside to our position in light of the fact that Sam had been the only family provider and, according to the financial affidavit he presented to the court two months earlier, where was the extra money needed to have the kids continue in the Jewish day school to come from?

The judge weighed in on our side, and said, "Unless you have income that you failed to disclose to the court, there is no money for the children's Jewish school tuition. I have no choice but to deny your motion and grant your wife's request to allow her to transfer the children to the Catholic school. If you can find the financial means to pay the Jewish school tuition, I will grant you another opportunity to refile your petition in the future."

But Sam got the last laugh. His parents offered to pay the tuition for the kids' Jewish educations and Debbie realized that her clever move wasn't so clever. This seemed to be the icebreaker as the two were so exhausted after going through this battle, they agreed on other matters and the divorce was finalized.

I hadn't had enough time to reach over and pat myself on the back for getting this couple to the peace table. The détente was quickly destroyed when the kids began bringing home tales of each parent's new loves and the anger that led to their original sex hiatus-cum-divorce reared its ugly head once more.

Debbie got me on the phone post haste as her anger boiled over. I suspect that phone lines were burning up between Sam and his attorney, too. Thus began a flurry of complaints and threatened court actions that had the potential to make me and the opposing attorney rich.

I went home and told my wife that it looked as though the two of us would be able to send our kids to a Jewish day school after all.

The Weight of the World

Howard was a successful divorce attorney. He met his wife, Susan, at a fraternity party while attending the University of Illinois. Many of the girls flirted with this six-foot, popular, young man.

The weekend party at the frat house was a typical one: horny dudes, girls seeking an MRS degree, loud music, and lots of beer. But the haze of the moment disappeared when Howard spotted Susan, introduced himself, and was quickly overwhelmed by her looks and sassy mouth.

Susan, studying to be an elementary school teacher, was funny and her retorts easily matched his verbal quips; so they found themselves in the kind of rhythm that couples seek that has the potential to go somewhere. She was fairly tall and quite curvy—Howard made that observation while catching glimpses of her tight jeans and sweater. Looks, check. Wit, double-check. Something clicked for them both.

The pair quickly fell into a mutually supportive team. Susan encouraged Howard to excel in his classwork and in turn, he treated her with respect and affection. She welcomed the attention and love, and she liked the fact that he was not an immature, spoiled, frat guy. They became best friends instantly and within a month, they were so inseparable, she moved into his room.

At the start of the following school year, the couple rented an apartment off campus and would stay there until they graduated. Susan loved to wear his big shirts around the apartment while studying and the two held hands when walking to class. There were plenty of hugs and kisses to go around and the sex was warm and wonderful.

After graduation, Howard enrolled at Northwestern University's law school and Susan found a teaching job in Chicago. The plan was to wait until Howard graduated to get married, but after a year, they decided to tie the knot at the Chicago Yacht club.

Howard used the occasion and champagne to tell friends and strangers that Susan was the best thing that ever happened to him, and the two of them seemed to fit this idyllic picture: after twenty-three years of married life and three kids off to college, they remained happily together.

Given the title of this book, you know I will eventually be invited into this story and, of course, that did happen for reasons that I see all too often. The older Howard got, the more attention he paid to his health and fitness objectives. His membership to a health club near his law firm was a budgetary priority and he prided himself on his youthful body.

Susan, on the other hand, admitted that taking a walk around the block was as much exercise as she wanted to get and you don't need me to draw you a picture of how things began to go downhill. Her weight continued to balloon.

Howard tried to be supportive, but he was no longer physically attracted to his former sweetheart. He felt guilty because he understood that her weight was at the heart of the issue and the way she looked had begun to set him further adrift. Opportunities to have affairs came his way, but he loved his wife and walked around 24/7 feeling conflicted.

If you're a proponent of the theory that it's the small things that lead to the biggest explosions, you will understand when I write that one night, he came home, spotted an ice cream container in the garbage and lost it.

"You are killing yourself. You are the only woman I have ever loved, but if you do not lose weight so we can go back to the way we were, I will consider a divorce." I wasn't there, but I understand she was as surprised by his outburst as he was when those words crossed his lips."

Susan's face grew ashen.

"Listen, money is not an issue!" he said, attempting to touch her arm in reaction to her recoil. "I love you. If you want to go to a weight-loss farm or spa for a month—have surgery—whatever it takes, just tell me and we'll make it happen. You will not have to do it alone. The weight is not healthy for you."

Howard's speech was a reality check for Susan, but it threw her for such a loop, she found herself eating even more, even exhibiting signs of addiction like sneak eating, hiding food, and yo-yo diets, each of which ended with Susan's anger and self-recrimination. Swearing the next "solution" would do the trick, she spiraled down rather dramatically.

Should weight gain be a marriage breaker? I see it all the time, though I often wonder how a couple that had lasted this long together was so fragile. It was literally and figuratively bending under the weight of Susan's eating. In the end, that's how I met Susan. Howard came to me to file for divorce and brought enough guilt with him to sink a battleship. As a result, he insisted on settling their financial issues without bloodshed. He did not want their dirty laundry aired in front of attorneys and judges he encountered daily.

In his eagerness to reach an equitable out-of-court settlement so as not to destroy his children, he bent over backwards to give in to her demands, most against my advice, but I knew how much he hoped that he and Susan could once again be friends. But Susan's attorney knew enough to identify and exploit Howard's guilt and the final divorce wound up costing my client more than it would have had we gone to trial.

A year later, Howard and I met up at a popular Chicago steakhouse for dinner so we could discuss his current financial status. As I was undertaking my usual risk-assessment profile while drinking a glass of wine, Howard looked up and stared. This wasn't like him. I turned to see what had captured his attention was a beautiful woman with a great shape, shoulder-length silky brown hair, and a certain familiarity that made me wonder if she was one of my clients.

He was obviously enraptured because I had to keep trying to get his attention so I could complete his financial assessment and enjoy what was left of my dinner. We managed to get through the evening, fought over who was going to write off the meal, and stood up to leave when I realized that Howard was heading in the direction of this stunning woman rather than following me to the exit.

You've probably already guessed that we were both looking at the new Susan. The gorgeous, slim, beautiful latest version of her had serendipitously wound up on a date that happened to take place at the same restaurant we had chosen for our business meeting.

I don't think it would be an exaggeration to say that I was floored and Howard was both shocked and mesmerized. My usually glib, carefree client had begun to stutter, but Susan immediately put him at ease by introducing her date and asking if we wanted to join them.

"She's not only gorgeous but gracious as well," I whispered when I finally dragged him away from her table. I had a hunch that he would likely be on the phone to her in a matter of hours, but for the moment, I just needed to make sure he was able to drive since the shocked look on his face remained.

As I drove home that night, I started to laugh, thinking that payback really is a bitch. Would Susan even consider seeing him after the awful blow he dealt her by saying, in sum, that she had grown too fat for him and that all of those years of love and affection had drowned in a sea of pounds?

She'll never take him back, I thought, knowing that the bets I make with myself are always doomed to fail, and once again, I was right: He did call and she did agree to meet and after sharing the story of having her stomach stapled and adopting a healthy lifestyle, the two of them started dating again.

I'll be honest: her girlfriends didn't get it. They agreed that the insult she had suffered was so profound, how could she ever trust that he wouldn't hurt her again? But, Susan just smiled. She sent Howard an e-mail inviting him over for dinner the next time the kids were in town. It was there that he learned that Susan was in a new and loving relationship and cared enough about Howard that she wanted him to know she had forgiven him.

Would this story have a happy ending if Susan hadn't been in another relationship? I guess none of us will ever know, but at least the two of them are back on a strong footing. Wish I could say that about all of my clients!

This Client
Suffers from Manopause

Michael worked as creative art director at a large Michigan Avenue advertising agency throughout his thirty years of marriage to Dana. He found that his home life was as successful as his business skills and was able to open his own agency at a fairly young age.

But, as Michael turned fifty-six, he morphed into the cliché-ridden stage attributed to most men when they start acting out of character: Dana diagnosed him as being in *manopause*.

This syndrome can take many forms. Some men chase skirts. Others buy cars with price tags equal to the price paid for their first homes. Michael suffered an eclectic type of manopause that rocketed him through a series of high-priced stages.

It began as exotic cars. Continued with his search to amass a collection of rare antique wristwatches and pens. He had a wine cellar built to accommodate a growing collection of wines that had begun to occupy every closet. When the guest room became a floor-to-ceiling wine repository, the contractor came to call.

Each new hobby brought that "first sex" thrill: The conquest. The acquisition. Time spent lounging in the world of the passion-of-the day. He began losing sleep after finding that some of the very best deals on whatever he was busy collecting could be found at all hours on the Internet from international resources. Sound like fun? It would have been—had Michael not tapped friends, family, and even his in-laws for funds to pay for his obsessions. Because "obsession" was the correct word to use describing his behavior, Michael became abjectly boring. He considered it his duty to educate everyone in his inner circle about his latest fetish, including long and tiresome monologues on how he bought, marked up, and profited from every deal.

Of course, these tales had an objective: Michael told his creditors that he would repay borrowed funds plus a share of the profits based on his highly successful track record. Michael told his investors (including Dana's parents) that it was essential they keep their financial dealings private because, in his words, "Dana is having some psychological issues and I don't want to worry her."

As Michael's obsession intensified, he needed more and more cash infusions to support his quests. The cash flow from the business that had kept his loans current with creditors dissipated at an alarming rate and as the business began to fail, he added bank business loans, business credit cards, and customer advance payments to keep him afloat. As moderate risks turned to more catastrophic ones, he stopped paying state and federal employee payroll taxes withheld from employees.

If you believe that things can't get worse, stop reading now, because Michael stepped up his travel schedule to attend auctions poised to help him add to his burgeoning assets. Meanwhile, Dana was left in the dark. When he told her he was off on a business trip, she assumed it had everything to do with his agency. What she didn't know was that the business was in steady decline due to his neglect; with employees running the show in his absence, the company's downward trajectory sped up.

It wasn't until Michael's client list had shrunk to new lows that he actually noticed how bad things had become and to add insult to injury, the 2008 recession hit and the advertising budgets for his remaining clients were slashed like paper fed into a shredder moving at warp speed.

I came into the picture at this point. It's not that Michael had realized the error of his ways and wanted to stop the bleed. The revelation hit home one morning when Dana found an IRS agent standing at their front door. He had come to inform them that their income taxes had not been paid for two years, and that number could grow to three in light of the fact that a third year of taxes was yet to be paid.

"You need to talk to my husband," Dana said, hands shoved into the pockets of her robe.

"We did, Ma'am. We've been writing letters and making phone calls to him for over a year but he neither acknowledges the letters nor returns my phone calls."

Dana was flustered. "You can reach my husband as his advertising agency. Can I get you the address?"

"I've just come from there. The address on file is an empty suite of offices. We asked around and learned that the business had gone under months ago."

"Well—where has Michael been going every morning when he packs a briefcase and leaves for work?" she asked, realizing the absurdity of her question as quickly as the words presented themselves.

The IRS agent shook his head, took a card from his jacket pocket, and handed it to her. "Please tell him that next time I have to come, it will be with a warrant."

The shock did some interesting things to Dana's system. She stuck the business card in her robe pocket and just sat down without moving, unconscious of the fact that hours were passing. Wrapping her mind around this huge revelation was proving to be impossible.

When at last she moved, her first act was to call Michael and leave an urgent message on his cell. As if to prove to herself that this moment in time was a product of imagination, she also did what she hadn't done for years: she called the office and was greeted by a familiar disconnection tone.

Hearing the panic in her voice, Michael raced home from the local wine auction he had been attending only to find Dana, still dressed in her robe. She grew hysterical so quickly, he could hardly make out what had happened to her, so she dug the card out from her robe and handed it to her.

I was Michael's next call.

Dana was in bed by the time I arrived to hear the details of this catastrophe from Michael's mouth. It was quite the goulash. As he unraveled his descent into hell, Michael took me through the odyssey. I'm not sure why he was surprised that I was so nonplussed.

"I hear stuff like this every day," I said. "What good would I be to you if I didn't have a clue about the types of financial crises people get into?" But there were some unique surprises, like putting the failing agency into Dana's name to qualify as a woman-owned enterprise to seek project orders and business from large corporations who had set aside funds just for using woman-owned businesses.

"Does Dana know that she owns a failed business?" I asked, intuiting the answer. "If you retain me to help you get out of this mess, you're going to have to tell her everything."

Like a schoolboy admonished about cheating on a test, he lowered his head. "Everything?"

I gave him the look I usually save for my kids when they ask a lame question.

Were there other surprises awaiting me as I put on my deep-sea diving equipment and plunged the depths of Michael's creative finagling? You bet. And before I could get too far into my audit, creditors of all types began to call Dana at home and on her cell phone, informing her of $600,000 in credit card obligations. Having been left in the dark for so long, she was shocked to learn that because the business was in her name, she was also on the string for unpaid employee payroll taxes.

What's a con artist to do when caught up in a financial tornado? Put his tail between his legs and disappear, leaving Dana to become the poster child for duped spouses. Having left me in addition to his wife, I voided our contract and like a hot football draft pick, I changed teams and recommended that she file for divorce.

Let's just say I wasn't able to retire from my practice after helping Dana limp through the two years it took to get out from under this debacle. There were times I became her psychotherapist. At times I turned into a suicide hot line. At nearly sixty, Dana was left in a situation that boggled even me, but she hung in there.

From his undisclosed location, Michael filed for both personal and corporate bankruptcy. The IRS received "married filing separate individual income tax returns" from Dana, so she avoided additional run-ins with the federal government.

In the end, everything was liquidated to relieve Dana's burden; so I also became a wine and watch liquidation specialist. At least this left Dana in a position to start a new life. I worked with several other attorneys by the time this mess was sorted out and in the end, we forced Michael to indemnify Dana if Michael failed to pay the income taxes owed.

Of course, Michael being Michael, he ignored those tax payments, too. More collectibles were held for auction by the bankruptcy court and, while I rarely do this much hand-holding, the twists and turns of this relationship wouldn't, in my opinion, ever end if we didn't make a few compromises, but on a fairly warm spring day in Chicago, Dana got her divorce.

"Don't feel sorry for me," Dana said firmly as we left the courtroom after having survived World War III in the trenches together. How could I help it? She wound up taking a $15-per-hour job and moving into a little apartment that didn't come close to the luxury home she had shared with Michael.

But she was free at last and even when she heard through the grapevine that Michael had managed to sweet talk a wealthy woman into marrying him, she laughed out loud. I had to agree with her when she called to give me the news of his newfound windfall: when the karma train finally pulls into his station, it's going to be ugly!

Boys Will be Bad

Sarah and Caesar worked together at
City Hall for several years and, amid the legendary intrigue and
games for which Chicago's municipal government was known,
their relationship blossomed.

Sarah was in her thirties and made no secret about the fact
that she feared that her chances of getting married and having
a family may have passed her by. In Caesar, she found a perfect
personality match, but as things got more serious, she also knew
she was tempting fate. As a Jewish woman, she could never imagine herself married to a Christian—much less have children with
him—and so she called off the romance and hoped that the two
of them could remain friends.

The news came as a shock to Caesar, who had no easy time
of it growing up. He credits high school basketball with keeping
him on the up and up; so he made decent choices and grades that
enabled him to pursue a college degree in political science from
DePaul University. He hoped to attend law school in the future,
and this impressed Sarah most of all.

Torn between her attraction to Caesar and her religious beliefs, Sarah continued to enjoy Cesar's friendship, wit, and company. Caesar proved to be a guy who didn't know the meaning of giving up; so he pursued Sarah despite her misgivings. Their friendship-turned-romance-turned-friendship again morphed into a friends-with-benefits relationship. Through it all, they flirted with the idea that there might be a future together—until the subject of religion reared its head, pushing Sarah back from the brink.

To say that Sarah was shocked when Caesar brought up the possibility of converting to Judaism is the proverbial understatement. His willingness to change religions was expressed on a Sunday morning as the two of them sipped coffee in bed. She literally spewed coffee on the sheets when he broached the subject.

"Do you have any idea how much time and study the process takes?"

"I'm willing to do it for you," he said sincerely.

Her mind scrambled to make sense of his willingness to undertake so serious a change in faith. But after Caesar agreed to her terms—that if, at any time, he found that Judaism wasn't a religion he was comfortable practicing, he could quit, no matter where in the conversion process he found himself.

At this point, things moved rapidly. Caesar honored his commitment, undertook conversion classes at a conservative temple, and one year almost to the day that Caesar offered to convert, his Rabbi married them. Honeymooning in Puerto Rico was more than just a chance to launch their marriage. She returned pregnant.

Over the first five years of marriage, they had three beautiful children and life was good. Caesar and Sarah proved loving spouses and parents and the family even attended Friday night Sabbath services weekly, sending the kids to Hebrew school.

Call me the consummate skeptic, but this much harmony, love, and goodness in a relationship is so rare, it's hard to wrap my head around. And, of course, I didn't have to. One night, Sarah was in bed reading when Caesar's cell phone began to ping.

It stopped, but re-started minutes later. She called out to him as he showered, but he didn't respond. She picked up his phone and read the messages after the third signal.

The three texts were of a sexually personal and private nature. She was so shocked, she couldn't move. When Caesar returned to the bedroom wrapped in a towel, he saw the panic on her face, looked at the phone, and immediately put two and two together.

Caught with his pants down, literally and figuratively, Caesar attempted to talk his way out of his jam, but once his brain caught up with his mouth, he knew he had no choice but to make a full confession. He had been having a frivolous affair. It meant nothing to him. "I swear, it won't happen again," he said lamely when there was nothing more to be said.

Swearing over the next few days that this had been his only affair since the day they married, Caesar knew that she held all of the cards. As for Sarah, she wanted to believe Cesar because she loved him and her children loved their father. Further, Sarah was afraid of the consequences a divorce would provoke.

To help her cope with this situation, Sarah began to ask herself what she could do to help mend their relationship, and while Caesar found great hope in her willingness to talk about how to fix things, a knock on the front door of their home one morning after he had gone to work put the brakes on the situation.

The stranger standing at her door didn't beat around the bush. "I'm carrying Caesar's child," she blurted out, nearly knocking Sarah off her feet. "I just found out and wanted you to know that I'm not the only woman he's been seeing." To prove her point, the stranger told Sarah that he had been very honest with her about not leaving his wife and he did tell her about the other affairs he had had.

There was no turning back. Sarah called me as soon as she dismissed the woman and closed her front door. By the time Caesar returned home that night, Sarah had acted on all of the advice I had given her:

—If you can't have the lock changed, make sure the chain is on the door so he can't get in.

—Have his bags packed.

—Talk to the kids and apprise them of the situation.

—Be prepared to inform him that you've instituted divorce proceedings.

It was a shock heard around the neighborhood when Sarah directed him to the garage where his suitcase awaited and suggested he chose from any of the women he had been consorting with to find somewhere to sleep for the foreseeable future.

"I'll have you arrested if you try to enter this house," she said. "I mean business."

As Sarah's divorce proceedings progressed, she was assaulted by questions that revolved around Caesar's conversion and her willingness to believe that just because he had become a Jew meant he would be faithful.

Given Caesar's infidelities, we didn't have much trouble making demands of him that he felt compelled to meet out of fear of being even more exposed than he already was. We got Sarah the home, interim maintenance, and child support. By the time we reached the end of the divorce proceedings, Caesar would be confronted by the results of his bad behavior: his lifestyle was going to face the dismal financial beating he deserved.

Did things get weirder after the pair divorced? Yes. Caesar returned to his church and insisted on taking the children with him on weekends he enjoyed visitations. We're not sure whether he was taking advantage of Sarah's strong religious beliefs to leverage reductions in his obligations or whether he had concluded that perhaps this was God's payback for him leaving the church!

The last straw came about when he enrolled the children in a Christian Sunday school. By now, Sarah had developed the armor of a Viking shield maiden: she wasn't having any part of it. His wild threats of having the kids baptized no longer held any power over her and she sought legal relief, presenting evidence to the court that Caesar's conversion and affiliation with their synagogue proved his intent to have their kids raised in the Jewish faith.

I hired a family psychologist to explain to the judge how much this infighting about religion was beginning to harm the kids in an already confused environment in which the children were trying to come to grips with their parents' divorce. She won. My thought? Nobody messes with the Chosen People!

Miracles do Happen

Nina's friends don't hold back when they offer opinions. They all named her worthless husband "The Schmuck," which is loosely translated to: The Jewish Asshole. The name stuck so well, none of them could recall his real name; and to be truthful, neither could I—a big problem when you're trying to reach back in time to gather material for a book; so for purposes of this tale, I'm going to refer to him as Bernie the Schmuck.

Bernie left Nina for another woman after she had given him those proverbial "best years of her life." The other woman wasn't Jewish, but Nina was devout, so she didn't consider herself free of Bernie despite the civil divorce I handled for her.

I don't have enough fingers to list all of the ways Bernie hurt Nina. Suffice to say that the hard feelings were mutual, yet he held all of the last cards because without a Jewish divorce, she remained religiously tethered to him. We tried every trick in the book to get him to acquiesce, but his perpetual response was,

"I'm not about to spend money on a Jewish divorce when my new wife isn't Jewish."

Being in limbo is never pleasant. I've had clients stuck in this situation before and in most of them, the man used the matter of the Jewish divorce as a battering ram. Bernie didn't care that Nina could never marry again in her faith and the two of them continued to wrangle over everything from support payments to this dicey issue.

For two years, Nina fought and pleaded with Bernie the Schmuck for the Jewish divorce. He grew weary of her pestering and finally told her that if she would agree to waive maintenance and child support, he would make arrangements with the Jewish court for the religious divorce.

It was rock and hard place time. Nina would lose regardless of her options; so she turned to her rabbi for what she hoped would be wise advice. The holy man could have appeared on a Rabbis Go Wild calendar page: he wore thick glasses, had an unkempt beard, and had the harried look of a man who had spent too much time reading the Talmud and not enough time on grooming or wardrobe selection.

"There are thousands of women just like you who are chained to husbands unwilling to grant them divorces," he intoned.

"Tell me something I don't know, Rabbi. I need a way to make this happen and put an end to this."

"I'll pray for you. Give me a couple of months to consider this."

"A couple of months?"

His look forestalled any further questions. And so Nina waited.

A month or so later, Bernie was walking to his car on a Chicago side street when a van stopped and the driver asked for directions. Going on at length about where to turn to reach their destination, Bernie was caught off guard as eight or nine young men in religious garb and wearing ski masks pushed him into the van.

He struggled mightily, but he was overwhelmed and outnumbered. His first thoughts reflected his worst fears: he was going to be held for ransom. His mind began to buzz as he contemplated who had the resources to make good on a kidnapping payout. Before the van was put into gear, one man put a gag in Bernie's mouth and slid a cloth sack over his head so he could see next to no daylight.

Arriving at the destination, Bernie was pushed out of the back of the van and the cloth hood was pulled from his head. He found himself in a nondescript garage and was summarily shoved onto an old wooden chair that wobbled precariously under the weight of his body.

That's when several of the men began beating his body with— and he swears to this day he didn't imagine this—black men's socks filled with coins. Overcome with pain and fear, he cried out and begged for his life, but from the looks of the garage, he had a better chance of being heard in China than in Chicago.

The beating was merciless. He continued to cry and swear— even offering his captives money to release him, but his assailants quickly grew weary of his pleading and stuffed a sock in his mouth (minus the coins). As he slipped in and out of consciousness, it suddenly dawned on Bernie that nobody had said a word to him.

That was about to change. A man walked into the room from a door behind him, and in the silence of the moment, those footfalls added an ominous sound to the already frightening scenario. The gag still in place, he could do nothing more than utter muffled grunts. At least with the addition of this guy to the room, the beating ceased.

Silence hung in the room like a clothesline of wet sheets on a windless day. When the man walked around the chair to confront Bernie, he finally spoke. "Schmuck," he said using the euphemism Nina's girlfriends had come up with, "Nina can remarry and be free from you if you voluntarily agree to a Jewish divorce and sign the papers that I have here."

Holy shit! Bernie thought. I'm not going to die.

The man pushed back his mask to reveal the face of an old Jewish sage. "If you don't grant her a Jewish divorce, she won't be free until you die. I'm giving you the choice to do the right thing. Don't respond to me until you choose your words carefully," at which point one of the men who had been beating him pulled the gag out of his mouth.

Bernie still felt as though he had control over the matter, looked at his captors, and in a cocky voice, taunted, "Old man, if you don't want my blood on your hands or to spend the rest of your life in prison, untie me now!"

When I heard the story second-hand from Nina, I couldn't decide whether Bernie was not just a schmuck but an idiot as well, but I do know that it was only seconds before coin-filled socks were again put to work as the harsh beating continued.

Nina says she knows it's wrong to smile when she recounts this story, but after what Bernie had put her through, she decided to stop apologizing for her response. I was spared the bloodiest details, but the sock patrol continued until Bernie had had enough. He knew he couldn't withstand much more. His captors brought a wet rag to clean up his hands so he could sign the document that was witnessed by one of the bystanders.

"You must respond to this question aloud," said the old man. "Are you voluntarily willing to give your wife a Jewish divorce?'

Bernie nodded his head. One of the posse lifted his bag of coins. "Yes! Just leave me alone; no more!"

When Nina received a call from the rabbi saying that Bernie submitted to a little of his persuasion and signed the paperwork, and agreed to granting her a divorce, she was speechless.

In a year's time she was remarried to a good man.

Section VIII

ALL Divorces
Require Difficult Decisions

The Value
of Good Communication

What happens when you find that your soul mate isn't the person you married? It creates a longing to escape with the person who lives in your heart.

Consider good friends Michele and Janet, who first met when their eldest children attended preschool together and they volunteered to be room mothers. There was an instant bond of friendship and trust that made them sisters. Additionally, they worked in the same industry, residential and commercial real estate, which added another element to their bond.

The relationship grew so close, they shared clothes, advice, and they took turns caring for each other's children. Their first morning phone calls were to their moms and then to each other. The secrets Michele and Janet shared were uncensored. Even their husbands weren't privy to all of them. And although their spouses both worked in Chicago's construction trade, the couples didn't socialize together. Both husbands had difficulty expressing love and emotion to their wives and children.

The two women carried on with their busy lives until one day, when recurring infections sent Michele to her gynecologist for a checkup.

"There are several possible reasons for your infection," the doctor said, as Michele perched atop the examination table dressed in her paper gown. "Either you're having an affair, your husband is having an affair, or your body may be responding to medications or hormonal changes."

"Well, I'm not having an affair; so you can take that off your list," Michele responded. Her doctor prescribed antibiotics to fight the infection and Michele, a master at denial, left without acknowledging the gorilla in the room: could her husband be having an affair?

Who to turn to? Not me, at this point. Michele immediately got Janet on the phone and the two agreed to meet for coffee. Janet wasn't shy about her suspicions and urged her friend to do a little sleuthing while Michele waited for her meds to do their work.

Of course, the nagging suspicion remained somewhere in her head and on a day she decided to stop by her hubby's office to take him out to lunch, she wasn't surprised when his receptionist offered to page him at the job site he was supervising that day.

"Don't bother," she said, "I'll surprise him." She stuck the piece of paper bearing the construction site address into her pocket and drove to the Lincolnshire location and parked on the street.

Unsnapping her seatbelt, Michele glanced across the seat and noticed two people locked in an unmistakable embrace. She had no trouble identifying her husband's silhouette once they moved apart.

As tears rolled down her face, Michele restarted the engine. She drove a block before calling Janet on her cell and telling her she was on her way to her house. Janet was busy with a client, but she sensed the urgency in Michele's voice and told her she would go home as soon as possible.

Michele used an emergency key to Janet's home to get in, but she only had to wait a few minutes for the garage door to open, signaling Janet's arrival.

At this point, Michele had dissolved into a stuttering mass of tears in Janet's arms. Once she calmed down a bit, she filled in the details of her drive to the construction site. Janet was speechless and didn't know what to say, but she did suggest giving it a little time before confronting Rick.

"You have yourself and two kids to worry about. Maybe this isn't what it looks like," she said, reaching for a plausible explanation. "Maybe he just presented his client with a huge bill for the work he's doing and she freaked out when she saw the bottom line, so he was calming her down."

Michele laughed for the first time at Janet's effort to calm her down. As she relaxed a bit, the two women discussed a course of action. Michele, it was decided, would meet Rick at a restaurant, so he couldn't just get up and walk out when she asked for an explanation.

Once at the restaurant, Michele asked Rick about his day. When he avoided mention of the Lincolnshire stop, she asked, "Who lives in Lincolnshire?" Rick smiled and feigned ignorance.

"I know about the Lincolnshire woman," she added.

Michele could tell that Rick was scrambling for response, but he was silent.

"The truth, Rick," she persisted. "No bullshit. How long have you been seeing her?"

Rick squirmed in his chair before slowly replying, "A couple of months."

"So, is there a future for our marriage—do you want to stay married? What about the kids?"

A great silence again hung over the table as sounds of conversation, utensils, and background music filled the vacuum.

"Well, I think that the best course of action is for you to go back to the house, pack your clothes, and move out for the time being—until you know what you want and what is important to you," she said. "Leave now and when I get home with the kids, I don't want to see you there."

Michele put on a brave smile when she went to pick up the kids from Janet's home, motioning toward another room so she could report on her meeting with Rick. Janet gave her as much confidence as she could muster, assuring her that she had done the right thing. The kids were sleepy but seemed to accept her explanation when she told them on the drive home that their daddy had to go out of town on business.

After they had left, Janet told her husband about her friend's dilemma, but he said little, turning over in bed to sleep. For a fleeting moment, Janet wondered if her husband had cheated on her as well, but quickly fell asleep.

Michele called my office before showing up at my doorstep the following day. She shared her story, said she wanted to file for divorce, though she admitted that she was willing to keep the door to their marriage open should Rick decide to try and work things out. I had my doubts. They were confirmed the next day when Michele called to tell me that Rick had moved into the Lincolnshire house.

I resisted the impulse to say, "Well, that's one way to avoid having to commute to work," but of course, I couldn't because Michele was relying on my professional help, not my wry wit. We moved forward with the divorce process more quickly as my client believed that moving in with his "friend" showed he had made his choice.

Not able to come to grips with the enormity of this situation, Michele spent the next two weeks consuming too much wine and she kept moving up the cocktail hour until it began in the early afternoon. Janet tried to be a good sounding board, but felt helpless. When Janet suggested a girl's weekend—a getaway for the two of them so Michele could clear her head away from the kids—she agreed to allow Rick to stay in the house with the kids during her absence.

"We're going to Vegas," Janet announced, holding up two

plane tickets. "If you can't forget what's going on there, you can't forget things anywhere."

Both women were able to relax once the plane left O'Hare. During the flight, both talked about their marriages and realized that their husbands were even more similar than they thought. Bottom line was that neither felt she had both a friend and a lover in their spouses and intimacy was almost nonexistent.

Janet admitted longing for a relationship that included a strong friendship and a great sexual match. She poured a glass of wine from the little bottle on her pull-down tray and said, "Michele, if I could find a man who was the male equivalent of you, I'd leave Richard in a New York minute."

As is the case with badly needed getaways, time flew by. The two enjoyed lots of pool time, margarita, and carefree dinners; as well as time spent at the slots where both of them surprisingly won more than they lost. When two guys tried to pick them up at the casino bar, they giggled and felt flattered. Neither was permitted to refer to the time left on their vacation because they truly didn't want the trip to end.

But, of course, it had to end. On the night before their departure, the two sat at the piano bar at New York New York drinking and singing as the pianist took their requests. When he began to play the song *Will You Still Love Me Tomorrow?* Michele spontaneously kissed Janet on the lips and said yes.

Was the kiss a single act of playful spontaneity or the result of deep-seated feelings that lay just below the surface waiting to bubble up? The answer came when the two of them returned to their hotel room and they fell into bed, where both had her first sexual experience with another woman.

Morning-after confusion is not the sole domain of heterosexual couples who tumble into bed after an alcohol-infused lovemaking session. The two were having issues sorting out their feelings. Each time one of them brought up the subject, it proved to be too volatile to deal with; so they moved onto other topics.

By the time they arrived at McCarren for their flight home, both knew that things between them had changed forever.

For the next couple of months, Michele and Janet returned to their familiar routines, seeing each other regularly and acting, for all intents and purposes, as though their Vegas trip existed only in so far as their non-sexual activities were concerned. But feelings, once uncovered, have a nasty habit of refusing to go back to where they dwelled in the past.

The catalyst proved to be when I stepped in and literally gave Michele the legal boost she needed to think seriously about her feelings for Janet. Her divorce settlement was a done deal and all of the monetary aspects were sorted out. She was free. Free to be with Janet if she wished.

I'm not sure why my clients confide in me about sensitive topics that have no bearing on their divorces, but they do. Sometimes I feel like a Jewish priest minus the confessional booth. I consider myself an enlightened person; so Michele's confession about making love with Janet wasn't the shock she feared and the last time I talked with her, I was sad to learn that while Michele was eager to explore her newfound sexual experience with Janet, her friend could not escape her conventional thinking and decided to remain with her husband for the time being, rather than explore "what could be."

As for Michele, she came to the realization that she is bisexual, open to relationships with either gender. In many ways, Janet had done her best friend the biggest favor of all: she was there to bear witness to everything from Michele's courage to end her marriage to their shared sexual experience.

Did the friendship end? From my perspective, it had changed so radically, both women would have to acknowledge it if they hoped to keep their loving relationship from stagnating. As for me, I do love happy endings; and for my client Michele, she got more than most at a fairly young age; so beginning life anew offered much promise.

Pay For Your Sins

John's one-bedroom apartment lacked a decorator's touch. It was a sad place for a sad man. From his window, he could barely glimpse Lake Michigan. He recalled living in such a beautiful home once; now, he couldn't get out of bed without aches and pains.

John was both a friend and a previous divorce client. The recession took a toll on his world: as a successful member of the U.S. furniture manufacturing industry and owner of retail furniture stores, John was the quintessential success story until the dominos began to fall. I went to bankruptcy court with him and stood by helplessly as the remainder of his once blessed life imploded and destructed.

In my opinion, some of us are born lucky. Others acquire their luck thanks to something (four-leaf clover, horseshoe, and assorted charms) or someone. Joy was John's lucky charm, and when she left him for another man, his loss moved from sadness to obsession. My opinion of Joy was somewhere in the middle. I could see her virtues and I could see her weaknesses. The second caused her to bail on John when his financial life landed in the dumpster and she jumped ship like overly leveraged investors during the stock market crash.

Their love story was typical of North Shore Chicago couples: her older brother Mark knew John and fixed the two up. From that moment on, they would have had to work on failing to lose the trajectory of success both enjoyed. He established his own company to represent furniture manufacturers and greatly increased the number of retail stores he served. In the end, he was involved in all aspects of the furniture industry.

Sure, travel was extensive—after all, North Carolina is Mecca for the furniture industry—but Joy was happy to stay home, decorate their own place repeatedly, and enjoy the good life that consisted of a country club membership and financial security. John was lonely on the road; so he took comfort from the women he met, then traveled home on the weekends to be with his family. Saturday morning golf game followed by a late-afternoon Sunday departure. Joy and the children would see John for three weeks around the Christmas holidays and weekends.

Acting as a single parent the moment John left, Joy handled all aspects of their children's upbringing. She missed John but knew that his success depended on his ability to shuttle back and forth between cities; so she had no reason to complain. He was happy to leave all decisions related to the kids to Joy, so he could focus on business.

Does this sound to you like a recipe for disaster? Once upon a time, I would argue that it wasn't, but the world has changed and I've grown more skeptical; so I saw this perpetual separation as a train wreck waiting to happen. I was just clueless whether it would be the Joy Express or the John Express that derailed.

Apologies, dear reader, for the travel analogy but I lead you in the right direction: Joy began to work in the travel industry as their kids reached college age and she had run out of decorating ideas for their home. She proved the ideal agent. She was organized, imaginative, and had a great personality that drew people to her.

Included in the perks of a popular travel agent were freebies: hotel stays, airfares, attractions, and extras. For those of you who don't recall travel before the Internet, once upon a time, travel agents were the only resources you could use to make travel arrangements. Joy was sitting at her desk one day when Mike, a widower of about the same age, ambled in looking for a getaway.

"Will you be traveling alone?" The question was standard.

"My wife recently passed away and I need some time to collect my thoughts now that all of the tasks involved with her death are resolved," he said.

"You've come to the right place," Joy smiled. For the next hour, she brought out so many brochures, photos, and itinerary sheets, his head began to spin. In all, Joy had filled his head with images of tropical islands, European hot spots, the Middle East, and the Pacific Rim.

"I don't think I'm looking for a reflective place, a place where I can think," he laughed.

"I've been invited to experience a brand-new Arizona spa in a week. This place is eager to attract guests. If I could interest you in it, I'm pretty sure they would be happy they invited me to check the place out."

"I thought spas were for women."

"Not anymore!" Joy enthused. "You can hike in the hills and the desert, get massages, eat great food, and there are side trips—like donkey riding, for example—if you want to walk on the wild side."

Mike was enchanted—both by the idea of the spa and the woman selling the property. He said yes and she booked his arrangements. To make sure that there were no misunderstandings, Joy added, "My husband misses out on all of these great trips because his work keeps him so busy. I have to experience them for both of us."

Due to the lateness of his booking at the spa, Mike may have

had his choice of new suites but Joy had to do a little maneu-
vering to get him a flight that wouldn't cost a fortune. "Are you
willing to layover in Denver to get a better rate?" she asked. That
was fine with him; and so the next time they saw each other it was
at the spa's outdoor dining room. She was talking with the sales
director and he didn't feel comfortable interrupting, so he waved.
The following morning he asked if he could join her for breakfast
and Joy said yes.

"What do you think of your accommodations and the service
thus far?" Joy asked, donning her travel agent hat.

"This was probably the best idea anyone has ever come up
with," he replied.

Joy laughed. "I'm going to take all the credit. I've already been
invited back. I'm the only travel agent on premises who actually
booked a guest before seeing this place. I'm glad you're pleased."

Joy neither wanted to interfere with the quiet contemplation
that Mike so obviously needed nor did she want him to think she
intended to pursue a personal relationship by latching onto him
like a stalker, so she cautiously kept tabs on him and waved whenever their paths crossed.

But, on one sunny afternoon, she encountered Mike sitting
on a bench, staring out at the hills and the sunset as if imagining
how his wife would love this peaceful place. There were tears
rolling down his cheeks, so Joy's compassion kicked in and she
approached him.

"Do you need to talk?" she asked tentatively.

He nodded his head.

"Want to take a walk?"

"Yes. I would like that."

The two of them set off on a walk that proved to be a mix of
chatter and silence. When Mike had relaxed into a comfortable
state, he said, "You have no idea how lonely I feel."

Joy stopped dead in her tracks. "Oh, but I do."

"I'm so sorry—I never thought to ask about your husband.
I saw his photo on your desk and you wear a wedding ring, so I
assumed he was still in the picture."

"Is that a pun?" Joy asked with a sad laugh. "Is he in the picture because his photo's on my desk?"

"I didn't mean it that way," he said with a questioning laugh. She could tell he felt comfortable.

To this day, Joy has no idea what prompted her to respond, "Believe me, I know what loneliness is despite being married for decades. My husband is married to his job and his golf game; so I've been forced to live like a single woman for the most part." She began to cry and felt ashamed. She was supposed to be comforting him.

Pulling herself together, she apologized profusely for her outburst, but in fact, her tears seemed to create a bond between them and he insisted on having dinner with her that night. "I'm buying," he said.

"But the meals here are included with your spa stay." She looked at Mike and realized that he was joking and she broke into a grin that spoke volumes about how relaxed she felt around him and at that moment.

That night's dinner proved to be one of the liveliest in her memory. The two of them talked nonstop about their lives, their kids, and their work. Each found a friend who understood their loneliness. By the time the two returned to Chicago, neither of them could imagine their relationship coming to an end, so they agreed to see each other as friends and confidantes but nothing more.

In my opinion, this friendship born out of lost love and empty hearts caused them to become frequent companions, enjoying dinners and movies together. Importantly, they acknowledged finding someone with whom they could share their inner feels and thoughts. Over the years, she felt like a widow with only the memories of weekend moments.

Joy longed for simple things, like hugs and hand holding. She eventually gave in to the physical attraction that had been brewing between them, and found the passion to be overwhelming. She felt guilty about being married, but knew, after a year, that she couldn't imagine life without Mike in her life. Fortunately,

John was so self-involved, he neither noticed nor commented when their infrequent marital relations dried up completely.

As I advised Joy, while we were talking about legal matters that revolved around her travel agency, she was playing with fire, but frankly, I'd never seen her look happier. What clinched the relationship and moved the love affair from hot to hotter came about when Joy was offered a trip to the Greek Islands from a new resort.

Giddy with excitement, she asked Mike to join her for the ten days. He was able to get away. Together in an idyllic paradise like Greece, where turquoise waters and perpetual sun made the world feel perfect, Mike found himself unable to continue sharing Joy with another. "I never want to leave, you or paradise," he said as they lay on the beach, her head on his chest. There was peace and comfort in his arms. He whispered his intent to her that he wished to marry her. She promised she would think about it.

Rather than wallowing in euphoria after a magical a vacation with Mike, Joy wasn't home for more than a few days before she realized that she wasn't cut out to live two lives with two men either. She either needed to leave her husband to be with the man she had come to love or find a reason to stay with her husband and end the affair.

Joy told Mike that she would have a conversation with her children and then with John. Mike prayed that Joy would choose his love because he didn't want to suffer the loss of his second great love.

I'm afraid that you're going to have to buy my next book to see how this puzzle was solved. Since I know you won't tell Joy what I think, I'm going to share my opinion with you: if a husband hasn't stepped up to the plate emotionally for twenty-five years, why would anyone with as much going for her as Joy settle for another twenty-five years in a loveless marriage?

Sometimes
a Prince is Actually a Frog

Greg was holding court at a party of twenty-somethings, regaling his audience with off-color stories and jokes. His bluster matched his physical size. He was a big man in all respects, but he never let his size determine his style; so when it came to his purchases, each was oversized—from his bright-red Corvette and his classic Harley Davidson, to his wardrobe selections. Let's just say you couldn't miss Greg if you tried!

Because Greg wasn't a good student in high school, he decided that college was not for him. Instead he used his over-sized personality and way with words to carve out a career in sales. It was a perfect fit. I noticed how outgoing and personable he was the moment I met him.

Sadly, his compelling persona turned on a dime every time the topic of his college-educated bosses came up. Greg had an Achilles Heel: he was jealous of them, calling them lazy, overpaid, and a couple of other descriptors I'd prefer not to add.

But Lori saw nothing of his envious side when she first met

Greg. Drawn to his over-the-top personality and confidence, she proved to be the perfect listener every time he railed against his bosses, commiserating with him and earning his confidence. He was, she concluded, a good and hardworking person and she was attracted to him on every level. Even his reputation for dating young woman and perpetually trading them in for newer models didn't bother her.

Greg noticed Lori for the first time at work as she sat in the breakroom chatting with office friends. He wondered how he had missed noticing her before; she was a tall, lanky, blonde, with a body that turned heads. On that day, he walked over to her and made small talk about the office, before switching topics.

"Ever ridden on a Harley Davidson?" he asked.

At first, she just tilted her head and looked quizzically at him.

"Sorry. Let me try this in English," he laughed. "Have you ever ridden on the back of a motorcycle?"

"Never. They don't look terribly safe to me."

"Depends on who's doing the driving," Greg responded. "I've got helmets. How about a test run? I'll tool around somewhere outside traffic, so you get a feel for the bike."

"Is this an invitation?"

"It is. Your bike initiation can come with dinner if you like."

Lori giggled. "I'll take you up on your test drive since you plan to feed me!"

The bait was set. Greg let Lori pick a day and their first outing proved better than he could have imagined. Unless you count the dinner conversation in which Lori informed Greg that it was her intention to stay celibate until she married.

Greg told me that nothing gets a guy's interest more than a woman who is absolutely sure she can resist sex successfully, particularly in light of the fact that she was obviously a passionate woman. They dated for three months and Greg tried his best to seduce her, despite heavy make-out sessions that left both of them in need of cold showers. Separately, of course.

Lori was forthright; so Greg couldn't say he had no clue where she stood. "It's hard to leave you when my body wants so much more," she told him and it was hard for him not to admire her tenacity. Throwing caution to the wind, he wanted to sleep with her so badly, he decided to propose to her. She said yes.

It was a short engagement during which time Greg was on his best behavior: charming, solicitous, loving, and attentive. His eyes were on the prize and they wound up at an Elvis-officiated ceremony at a Las Vegas chapel attended by their parents. Greg's folks were so delighted he had found the right girl, they gave the couple a check for a down payment on a new home.

Was he happy now that he had gotten laid? Not exactly. He turned his passion into the house they bought, insisting that one of the bedrooms be turned into his man cave, where he could keep his automotive publications and Harley memorabilia showcased. Lori didn't mind. They had three bedrooms, so there was space to share.

Once the glow had receded, Greg began to show his true nature. He showed signs of irrational jealousy whenever they socialized and he caught a glimpse of her conversing with men. He started walking over to her, putting an arm around her shoulder, and introducing himself as her husband if he didn't know the guy with whom she was talking.

At first, Lori loved hearing him tell the world that he was her husband—but once the two got home, he began to rail against these encounters, claiming that these guys were standing too close to her for comfort. It took no time at all before he started to question her wardrobe choices each time they were about to go out.

"Maybe you should change that shirt," he suggested. "I think it's a little provocative."

"Seriously?" she responded when he first began to make these comments; then she'd shrug and replace the shirt with something more conservative. But as his rhetoric stepped up to include just about every move she made that displeased him, Greg's behavior became obnoxious to Lori. His latest dictate? She wasn't to go into his man cave, even to clean it.

At this point, Lori knew she was pregnant, and she hoped that the news might mediate his behavior. She enjoyed a brief hiatus before his "evil twin," as Lori began to call his irrational moods, kicked in. And like most women married to controlling men, she kept expecting him to change.

The couple had two children in three years. Since Greg controlled every aspect of their lives, Lori felt trapped. Greg turned out to be a lousy father and left all parenting responsibilities to Lori. Understanding his power over her on a very visceral level, Greg let down his final walls and began to hit her when he felt she wasn't paying proper attention to him.

Trapped, Lori hadn't the will to seek help. As long as she had long-sleeved shirts in her dresser to hide the bruises he inflicted, the world knew nothing about what went on behind closed doors. She trusted her parents and her cousins, but they lived in Cleveland and were too far away to do much more than listen to her. She suspected her family would encourage her to leave Greg—just the thought of which was paralyzing.

And so, the family continued on in this self-imposed prison. Greg mentioned wanting another child. She had no idea why, since he ignored the two they already had and she loathed having sex with him. She took birth control pills to make sure she didn't get pregnant again and hid the truth from him, knowing that alone could have consequences if he found out.

Does anyone know why the smallest of actions are enough to turn the tide when a situation is as serious as Lori's and Greg's had become? I sure don't. But when Lori called me the morning after Greg had come home in an angry mood over a dispute with a customer, she confided that Greg blamed her for the customer's accusation. He demanded that she apologize for the incident that caused him to lose thousands of dollars in commissions, grabbing and shaking her until she did what most victims do when they're trying to survive: she begged for his forgiveness. But this incident had turned a switch in her brain. Despite his morning-after apology and promise never to touch her again, Lori wasn't willing to take another day of abuse.

She called me for legal advice and I counseled her on taking immediate steps: filing for an immediate restraining order, having the locks changed on the doors of their home, packing up his clothing and leaving it in the driveway. If his rage the night before was bad, it was nothing compared to finding his bags in the drive.

Lori had bought herself a little time by changing the locks, but she knew she had to do more. By the time the kids were ready to be picked up from school, she had packed their belongings, called her family, and made arrangements to come home. I would handle all of her divorce matters in Chicago, and the distance would protect her even more than the police could were she to stay in town and allow Greg to be within punching distance of her nose despite the court-ordered directive.

I always counsel my clients to put distance between themselves and their abusers if possible. In Lori's circumstances, she was able to do so quickly. She had no job. She had a place to go. And she needed to be safe. To this day, Lori calls me to tell me how wonderful her life has been since she left Greg and she's even come to joke about her former belief that celibacy was the way to go before marriage.

"You've discovered the Frog Principle," I told her. "Sometimes it takes sex to trigger the true behavior of a human being."

"So, I should have jumped into bed with him to uncover his inner frog? I don't think so. It was in my nature to wait for marriage to have sex. I think the lesson here is that things moved too quickly because Greg wanted to seduce me more than he wanted to make a good marriage."

A few days after our conversation, I received a big rubber frog in the mail from Lori. It makes a great conversation starter when I talk to my clients about their unique divorce dilemmas!

There is Always Hope for Love

Sarah was the smart egg in class. She understood the assignments and logically applied principles, coming up with answers to the instructor's questions that were clever and insightful. During her senior year at Ohio State University, she met Luke, a fellow high achiever who had no problem remaining in the upper ten percent of their graduating class.

Luke had lofty ambitions that required him to maintain a stellar grade point average: he was hoping to be accepted to one of the upper tier law schools he had set his sights on. Frankly, every time he listened to Sarah in class, he was both inspired by and attracted to her mind. Already aware of the fact that he could use a tutor to help him get through classes that didn't come easily to him, Luke honed in on her as the perfect candidate.

"I like to think that I'm not terribly dumb," he said, sliding next to her in the lecture hall. "But I'm so impressed by your understanding of the subject matter in this class, I was wondering if I could ask you to help me study for this class."

Sarah was taken aback. "You need a tutor?"

"Sort of." He grinned the grin that had been proven disarming to women over time. "I thought perhaps I could pay you for your time by taking you to dinner at Woody's Tavern."

She was flattered and interested. They agreed to meet for dinner that night at 5:30 p.m. Upon entering the eatery, Sarah had transformed herself from her usual plain-Jane jeans and nondescript shorts into a butterfly. Even her usual ponytail had been styled into a long and glamorous look. All that was left of Schoolroom Sarah was the signature purple backpack that she carried everywhere.

Luke awaited her at the bar, ordering their beers and pizza after she arrived. Since it would take an hour to get the pie out of the oven on this busy night, they had a second beer and chatted about shared interests that ran the gamut from films to music and food. Sarah told Luke she would be happy to help him; so after dinner, while it was still light out, the two made their way to the campus library, found a vacant study room, and began to discuss the current module the class had been assigned.

Luke found Sarah not just attractive, but also a skilled teacher. She was patient and used lots of examples and analogies to walk him through some of the material that seemed to elude him.

"You're good," he enthusiastically told her after realizing she was doing a better job of teaching him the material than the wizened old guy lecturing ad nauseam at the whiteboard to the accompaniment of slide after slide.

She blushed. "I'm happy to help."

"If there's anything I can do to repay you, just ask."

Although the beers had worn off, Sarah felt empowered enough to respond, "Friday night, how about taking me to Ugly Tuna Saloona for dinner? The music there is great." At that moment, it dawned on her that Luke could have a girlfriend— even a wife! "I'm sorry. I didn't mean to be presumptuous."

He caught her drift. "Sure, that sounds like a great way to spend a Friday night since I'm totally unattached."

She breathed a sigh of relief. "Want to meet me at my apartment around seven?"

"You bet," he said, scrambling through the papers on the table to find one on which she could write down her off-campus address.

On Friday evening, they drank, ate, and talked for hours. Sarah asked Luke to walk her home. As the intoxication of their intimate conversation lingered, they wound up having sex on the floor of her living room. The following morning, Luke caught sight of her in the shower and was captivated by her olive skin, exotic dark eyes, and sexy curves.

As smoothly as blending a frozen brick of ice cream into a creamy milkshake, Sarah and Luke fell into a serious relationship born of their intellectual and sexual compatibility, becoming virtually inseparable over that year. As a matter of fact, Luke told me his academic record improved even more thanks to the stability of their relationship. He got into his first law school of choice.

While Luke used his finance undergraduate degree and law school to craft a solid foundation for his future—one he hoped would focus on sports franchise law—his and Sarah's relationship stayed constant despite the fact that both of them were so academically swamped—she was getting her MBA—they frequently went days without seeing each other.

Ultimately, money became problematic. Even together they couldn't come up with enough for apartment rent and living expenses, and Sarah was beginning to push for a wedding ring; so Luke was faced with a choice that had no happy outcome, regardless of the road he chose: live with his parents to attend law school in Chicago, take a job that would force him to put off his law school graduation, or end his relationship with Sarah.

He chose his dream and cried when they broke up. Although she did offer to change schools and move to Chicago just to be close to him, he told Sarah he thought it would be best to part ways temporarily so each could focus on their careers.

Once Sarah finished her studies, she received a job offer with a big-box store to work at their corporate headquarters in

Cleveland. She dated occasionally, but was wary of relationships after her break-up with Luke. They communicated occasionally by e-mail. At first, he responded instantaneously, but the Northwestern School of Law curricula was daunting and over time, he stopped answering her messages in a timely manner.

By the time Luke graduated, Sarah was happily ensconced in her job. Luke had earned all of the credentials he needed to focus a practice on the subject he loved: sports contracts, tax law, and negotiations. His finite approach to his specialization proved a winning combination and he was hired by a firm with a reputation for excellence.

As fate would have it, Sarah's responsibilities included endless amounts of travel to evaluate store operations and management, and as something of an undercover spy for the corporation, it was almost impossible to make friends, even with the employees with whom she came into contact on a regular basis.

Now free of his daunting student schedule, Luke decided to risk rejection by reconnecting with Sarah. Facebook proved the ideal conduit and it took next to no time to re-ignite their spark. Sadly, it took the death of Luke's father to get the pair together. When he texted her about his dad's death, she asked for details, took a few days off work, and flew to Chicago without Luke's knowledge, showing up in time for the graveside service.

The moment Luke spotted her, he was overwhelmed. He later told me that though he had been crying on and off from the moment he heard of the heart attack that led to his father's death, seeing Sarah turned him into a sprinkler head! They clung to each other like lost children throughout the next few days as Luke took care of matters related to his father's estate. By the time everything was tidied up, they knew they could no longer bear to be without each other.

Like a cold, wet slap in the face, the real world called as Sarah told Luke she had to be in San Francisco the following day, having already taken more time off than she had intended.

"I have to be in San Francisco tomorrow and I've booked my ticket," she told Luke over dinner that night.

"So, how long will you be there?"

"About three days," she answered.

"How about dinner day after tomorrow?" he smiled.

"Don't you listen? I'm in 'Frisco, silly!"

"I can get a plane ticket, too," he said.

"What about your job?" Sarah had no idea why she was ruining this perfectly romantic moment.

As the story goes, they met up in San Francisco, where they strolled Fisherman's Wharf and where Luke got down on one knee and proposed, leaving Sarah speechless. (Guess who got to perform the marriage ceremony a few weeks later?)

After the couple returned to the Midwest, plans were made for Sarah to transfer to a job in Chicago that would, for all intents and purposes, bring their relationship full circle.

"Better late than never," Sarah said as the two of them recited their wedding vows on another pier—in this case, Chicago's Navy Pier.

"I think we have a theme here," Luke said, planting a kiss on her lips, after I pronounced them man and wife.

It is my earnest hope that I never get a phone call from this couple in which the word divorce is mentioned. According to my couple's radar, if this couple can't make a long and happy marriage, nobody can. They've renewed my faith in the possibility that love lasts forever.

The Doctor is In

As a kid, Lori was the quintessential tomboy, excelling at baseball, basketball, and golf. While other girls played with dolls, she was playing catch with the neighborhood boys. By the time she reached twelve, her father bought her a set of golf clubs and enrolled her in golf lessons. Growing up, most all of Lori's friends were boys.

Lori's golf game was so good, she proved a formidable opponent, regularly driving her ball over 150 yards and impressing just about every male golfer who admired her swing and her technique. Rather than being intimidated by Lori's skills, Michael found himself in awe—even when she beat him.

Was this a romance on the green waiting to happen? Not really. Lori and Michael were both kids every parent dreams about: focused on achieving great things and establishing priorities to achieve professional goals.

Fortunately, after Lori was accepted into Northwestern University's accelerated medical school program, she was able use her favorite sport to minimize the stress students in this daunting program often experience. When there wasn't enough time for 18 holes—or nine for that matter—she grabbed her basketball and devoted herself to some hoops time.

On this particular afternoon, she scampered solo across the court, in hopes another student might come along to give her the competition she craved.

A voice interrupted her concentration. "Don't I know you?"

Lori didn't turn around until she made her shot. When she did, she laughed, "Is this your best pickup line?"

He shrugged and started to walk away. She ran over to him, to get a better look at the dude she had just insulted, planning to apologize for hurting his feelings.

"Michael?"

"That's me. The guy you soundly beat at golf years ago. I see you've gotten a bigger ball."

She laughed. "C'mon. Join me!"

"So you can beat me at this, too? Do I look like a masochist?"

"Look at me—I'm a vision in my sweaty t-shirt and my hair is plastered to my head," Lori joked. "Do I look like someone who could vanquish you?"

"Okay," he said, placing his backpack on the ground. "I have ten minutes to beat you before class starts."

Michael towered over Lori, but she fought like a banshee, retrieving loose balls like a pro and nailing most baskets. She could easily out run him, but decided she would rather leave him with some self-respect so she did something unusual: she let him win.

"Gotta go," he said, wiping his face on his sleeve and picking up his backpack. "How about I take you to dinner for letting me win?"

Lori grinned. "I didn't let you win, but I never turn down a dinner invite. Give me your phone." She programmed her cell number into his device and waved. "Call me. We'll sort out our schedules."

It took a week to find a time when both of them were free, but when, at last, they met at a nearby pub, their short dinner turned into one of the longest meals either of them could remember having. As they were both in accelerated programs—Michael was planning to be a trauma doctor and she was intent on a career in medical management and bio-medicine—they had barely scratched the surface when the bartender issued a last call.

"How long have we been here?" Lori asked.

He checked his watch. "Long enough to join the kitchen staff," he said. "I want to see you again. We've got lots more to talk about."

Lori was pleased. Thrilled, in fact. The two of them seemed to be a perfect match and it took no time at all for Lori and Michael to settle into a routine that consisted of eating, playing, and helping each other with their studies. The brainiacs didn't suffer from a lack of sex; both fell naturally into this aspect of their relationship with the gusto they exhibited on the court and the golf course.

Things looked serious when it came time to play "Meet the Family," traveling to Arizona, where Michael's parents lived and becoming regulars at Lori's parents' holiday dinner table in Chicago. Was marriage inevitable? According to Michael's sister, she proclaimed the pair soul mates. As an homage to their early introductions, the couple married at her parent's country club overlooking the golf course.

As most Jewish families tend to do, both began hinting at grandchildren not long after the pair honeymooned, but this perfect story took a decidedly serious turn when, after a few years, Lori and Michael decided that their careers were stable enough to get pregnant. Instead God threw them a curveball: Lori went to her gynecologist for a full exam; tests concluded she was in the very early stage of cervical cancer.

Given their medical education and backgrounds, the two of them sought other opinions. Michael remained loving and reassuring as he perused copy after copy of medical test reports, contacted leading cancer hospitals and institutions throughout the U.S. and abroad. Eventually the two decided on a plan: her eggs would be harvested and frozen as she underwent a radical hysterectomy and follow-up treatment.

This was an ideal plan. Knowing her eggs were frozen gave Lori the confidence to believe that she would fight the cancer with as much gusto as she competed on the court and look forward to having children down the road via a surrogate.

Given this much emotional upheaval, the idyllic relationship Michael and Lori shared morphed into a clinical one. Michael approached Lori as her doctor, not her husband. He was reassuring and a constant presence, but what was missing from the relationship was the intimacy and tenderness she had come to rely on at a time when she needed it most.

Things came to a head one night when he rebuffed her sexual advances, saying he was too tired. In her eyes, he was rejecting her outright because she was no longer a whole woman, but rather than confront her fears, she began to curse and scream at him, grabbing her pillow and heading for the guestroom.

Michael didn't know what to do at that point; so he left her alone, figuring he would just exacerbate the conflict if he joined her in the guestroom. It was a dumb move, to be sure, but who can take back a moment in time and change a response?

Lori called her mom the following day and poured out her heart. But no matter what she said, Lori's emotions were too raw to allow her to think rationally. When her mom suggested therapy, she would have none of it and when she found out that Michael and her mother had talked about what to do to help her through this crisis, it made her even madder.

The schism between them continued to grow. Lori focused on her recovery and her work, going days without seeing Michael. For his part, he had run out of answers and patience. He understood what she was going through biologically, but she seemed oblivious to the mental state that now dominated her persona. Once Lori was out of danger, she moved into an apartment of her own to give the two "space."

When Michael first contacted me, it was for legal advice rather than a divorce, but I could tell from the get-go that this was where this formerly blissful, perfect couple was headed. "Have you tried getting her some counseling?" I asked. This was a standard question I asked clients and, frankly, if ever a couple needed to be in therapy, they did.

Brilliant people often make stupid decisions when their emotions are concerned. Michael made one stab (at my urging) to get Lori into couples' counseling, but I suspect his request was rather halfhearted as the schism between them had grown deeper than the Grand Canyon at this point. For all of her smarts and practicality, Lori had come to look upon herself as an infertile woman with a husband incapable of compassion. She felt abandoned and found solace only in her work.

The divorce was inevitable. I'm always sad to see couples who were obviously so compatible in so many ways, split up, but Michael and Lori had both radically changed as a result of her cancer diagnosis. Some people can handle a catastrophic disease and some can't. I suspect that Lori and Michael both felt betrayed by the science that had brought them together and the breakdown in their relationship was inevitable.

From the perspective of my involvement, the dissolution was fairly simple. There were no children to be considered and both of them had thriving careers that meant money wasn't at the top of their list of issues that needed to be hashed out.

Do I enjoy the occasional divorce that's full of vitriol, anger, and hostage taking (that's what I call parents who use their kids as red meat)? Not especially. Call me a hopeless romantic, but when I work with a couple as obviously compatible as Lori and Michael were, my usual reaction is sadness that I couldn't do more to help them resolve things beyond providing them with a legal conduit to end their relationship.

Section IX

It's All About the Money, Honey

Secrets and Lies

Don makes a living by networking ideas
and people, taking commissions or a piece of the action in return
for his services. You might call him a commercial matchmaker;
instead of fixing up couples, he acts as the middleman for lucrative deals.

For example, Don introduced investors to inventors and facil-
itated licensing agreements. That's how I met him; he needed
legal help handling the sometimes complex financial contracts
that required scrutiny. My credentials appealed to him.

For all of Don's wheeling and dealing, his wife, Nancy, was
his polar opposite. A TV actress, she played the role an Italian,
Catholic mother always eager to give the shirt off her back to her
children. In real life, Nancy wasn't very different from the character she played: she liked to spend big on her kids and grandkids.

Remember what I just said about this pair being polar oppo-
sites? It's true. But they shared one commonality: neither was shy
about risky spending; so while they appeared successful on the

outside, dollars flew out the door like swallows returning to Capistrano. By year's end, they often scrambled to borrow money for their taxes. Was it always like this? No. Once upon a time, they were more responsible in terms of spending.

Perhaps the area in which Don and Nancy were most vulnerable were their kids. Don even started a business for his eldest son and namesake, and he brought a nephew in to help run the tech enterprise that was set up to help business owners find appropriate software, update hardware, and troubleshoot computer and system glitches.

The idea? Brilliant. Every customer would be assigned to an exclusive tech, available and on call 24/7, so a bond was created that promoted loyalty and a high degree of immediate service to clients whose bottom line could be destroyed by a system crash.

Don was so certain that Junior's idea would be a smashing success, he financed it with credit cards and even went to the bank to guarantee business start-up loans so the boys would be properly capitalized the moment they opened their doors. He even hired someone to do their business plan and built salaries into it from day one.

Sound too good to be true? I thought so, too, when I learned after the fact that it was a done deal. Why did I react so dramatically to the news? When I discovered that both Junior and his cousin were coming into the business with no experience and two-year degrees in computer science from the local community college, let's just say I was speechless.

Funded with an investor's money, they opened up and, with no practical experience to speak of, the first thing they did was hire Mary, the woman Junior was dating. Junior was in love with her. Everyone thought Mary was the perfect first staff choice she had limited skills and she was affordable. Too bad she had no business experience and was more interested in looking hot than working.

Junior wasn't about to criticize or come down on the girl he loved and intended to marry; and as for Mary, she began pushing for a wedding date now that she was "part of the family business." Like most events in Don's and Nancy's world, everything about the wedding was over the top, from the showers and the parties to the wedding itself.

Allow me to describe the generosity of Junior's parents. When the bride-to-be told the couple that her parents couldn't afford a lavish affair, they did what they usually do: offered to foot most of the bill. With an open checkbook at this point, Mary went a little crazy and, by the time the bouquet was thrown and the horse-drawn carriage took the newlyweds to their hotel, the final tab came to over $300,000.

Don and Nancy had used $290,000 from their home equity line of credit (Mary's parents contributed about $10,000) to settle up the bills as Don looked for ways to snare new clients to help underwrite his newly enlarged state of indebtedness, and like most houses of cards, the honeymoon both literally and figuratively brought it down. During a heated argument at the end of the honeymoon, Mary told Junior that she'd been sleeping with another guy and married him only because it was too late to back out.

I heard this news when Don invited me to lunch a few weeks after the couple returned.

"How's the blissful couple?" I asked, lifting my water glass in a mock toast.

"They need a divorce attorney," Don responded. His face was ashen. I had to resist the urge to throw some water on his face to bring him around. I didn't know what to say.

"It's bad. Mary bought a car just before the wedding and Junior guaranteed the note because Mary's credit score was so low, she couldn't have financed a toy car. She also talked Junior into using all of the cash they got as wedding gifts to pay off her bad debts so they could start off fresh."

I lifted my hand as the waiter approached us. "Let me buy you a drink," I said. Don ordered a double.

"It gets worse. She's been sleeping with another guy. They

got into an awful fight the night before they were to return from the honeymoon when he asked her to promise that she would work harder on her spending issues. Her response was, 'I never should have married you!' She went on to throw the other guy's name into the mix." Don took a deep breath. "So you see why he's going to need more than financial advice."

I'll be honest. My initial thoughts were that the apple doesn't fall far from the tree. Neither Don nor Nancy were the world's best examples of fiscal responsibility, and it didn't help that Junior and his siblings rarely heard the word no when they tapped their parents for cash to underwrite their latest project, scheme, or idea.

Junior was indeed a hot mess because, in addition to having his albatross wife hanging around his neck—when she wasn't cuckolding him, that is—his business, the one he launched with his dad's money and his cousin's help—was also on a downward trajectory that resembled a rapid-flow toilet vortex.

I probably don't have to tell you that the wrangling involving Junior's interests required every bit of my legal and financial forensics training. I had to get him out of the marriage, find a way to put him on some sound financial footing, help resolve that drowning business issue, and I had to do all of this knowing that all of my hard work could be moot in light of the family's propensity for irrational behavior.

But, I said to the mirror every time I dressed to deal with some aspect of this family drama, that's why they pay me the big bucks. I've no idea where they got the money to pay my bills, but they did. Is there a happy ending to this story? Just the usual. Mary tried to wring cash out of a turnip after we bankrupted the company and made life so miserable for her attorney that it took over a year to sort things out.

In the end, Don came up with some cash so Junior could buy a small house. He got a dog instead of a new girlfriend, having had his fill of women for the moment. When I last saw Don, he told me Junior had been cured of the urge to launch a new business and was happily collecting a salary troubleshooting computers for a firm that saw his potential and was encouraging Junior to get some more education to reach his full potential. He sees a therapist twice a month, and is beginning to understand how his loving but somewhat irresponsible parents set him on his self-destructive path.

I'm not his father, but I feel a sense of pride when I see how much progress this kid is making. In my eyes, Junior has the potential to break the pattern. And that's a good thing.

Money Foolish

In his day, Bill was the most popular politician in the State of Illinois. Supremely conscious of his image, he abstained from alcohol and gambling, served as a high-ranking member of the Illinois government, and he almost become a United States Senator.

Bill was a friend to the small businessman. He helped many restaurants and construction companies obtain state contracts and settle disputes with the taxing and licensing arms of government. For his personal assistance, the businesses would hand Bill envelopes containing money and other favors. The cash gifts were placed in bank safety deposit boxes. It seems Bill's Achilles heels were women and money.

Because of his propensity for having a more than passing interest in the fair sex, Bill hired staff based on beauty and youth. Case in point: a sexy receptionist that gave him more good reasons than not to show up every day at her desk. He didn't have to work too hard to get her attention as she was smart enough to understand that power was everything, thus she was receptive to his advances.

The two of them began to go out for drinks and, on one of these occasions, he leaned over and whispered that he was about to go to Jamaica for business and relaxation. "How would you feel if I asked you to join me—just the two of us?"

She seductively bit her lip and touched his leg as she affirmatively nodded her head. In her mind, she was already envisioning what it would be like to replace Bill's current wife. She pursued him with gusto, using her youthful energy and good looks to corral his interest. It wasn't long before he offered her an expensive Lake Shore Drive apartment as an incentive to become his full-time guilty pleasure.

She was to be exclusive property. He, on the other hand, had other lady friends, and his most intimate friends had no clue how he managed to juggle so many relationships while his wife apparently remained clueless and under the impression that her husband was so important, he had to work day and night to handle everything. But Bill grew careless as a direct result of having become too cocky and smug. Telltale signs on the clothing his wife took to the cleaner's proved his undoing.

In one fell swoop, Bill's wife retained me to represent her. Using the time he was away from home to dig up what evidence she could find, and thanks to the private investigator I hired on her behalf, we were shocked to see the extent of Bill's deception. Frankly, I wondered how the man managed to find time to work in light of all of the secrets and lies we unearthed.

I don't like to brag—but I will—by the time we got Bill into divorce court, we were locked and loaded. Thanks to her willingness to spend some of his money on the investigators that were needed to paint an accurate picture of his philandering, we dug up all kinds of goodies, including safety deposit boxes that we managed to get court orders to open. One box alone was stuffed with $39,900 in fairly small bills.

Bill told her that these monies were campaign funds and

could not be used for personal expenditures; so he demanded that the court return the monies to him. In fact, we were able to prove that the only campaign funds this treasure trove covered were Bill's campaigns to finance his travel and the women in his harem. Since the funds weren't disclosed on income tax returns, the case against him just kept getting bigger.

Was Bill willing to stick with the fight? Yup. He was that foolish. He put up a fight over everything from the extra money his wife sought for child support to the maintenance her attorney had proposed. From my perspective, the guy was functioning in some sort of alternative universe.

Given the fact that Bill had been such a public figure for so many years, the Chicago press had a field day with this story, extracting as many salacious details about the many lives he was leading as possible and splashing them across the pages of the city's and suburbs' publications. Bill's exploits even made national news and when, at last, he was forced to give up because we had so much evidence against him, it wasn't a matter of if he was going to jail but when. We heard rumors that a Hollywood producer was going to make a movie about him!

I didn't care. I had gotten my client just about everything I could squeeze out of their assets. On the day the divorce was sorted out, none of the hotties he had romanced bothered to show up to render aid and comfort. The feds were waiting to arrest Bill on income-tax evasion charges and while it's not my practice to act anything other than professional, I couldn't help but roll my eyes as I saw handcuffs slapped on his wrists.

Made in the USA
Charleston, SC
22 December 2016